Supporting creativity and imagination in the early years

Supporting early learning

Series Editors: Vicky Hurst and Jenefer Joseph

The focus of this series is on improving the effectiveness of early education. Policy developments come and go, and difficult decisions are often forced on those with responsibility for young children's well-being. This series aims to help with these decisions by showing how developmental approaches to early education provide a sound and positive basis for learning.

Each book recognizes that children from birth to 6 years old have particular developmental needs. This applies just as much to the acquisition of subject knowledge, skills and understanding as to other educational goals such as social skills, attitudes and dispositions. The importance of providing a learning environment that is carefully planned to stimulate children's own active learning is also stressed.

Through the series, readers are encourage to reflect on the education being offered to young children, through revisiting developmental principles and using them to analyse their observations of children. In this way, readers can evaluate ideas about the most effective ways of educating young children and develop strategies for approaching their practice in ways that offer every child a more appropriate education.

Supporting creativity and imagination in the early years

Bernadette Duffy

Open University Press
Buckingham • Philadelphia

Open University Press
Celtic Court
22 Ballmoor
Buckingham
MK18 1XW

email: enquiries@openup.co.uk
world wide web: www.openup.co.uk

and
325 Chestnut Street
Philadelphia, PA 19106, USA

First published 1998
Reprinted 2000, 2002

A catalogue record for this book is available from the British Library

ISBN   0 335 19872 4 (hb)   0 335 19871 6 (pb)

Library of Congress Cataloging-in-Publication Data
Duffy, Bernadette, 1958–
    Supporting creativity and imagination in the early years / Bernadette Duffy.
    p. cm. — (Supporting early learning)
    Includes bibliographical references (p.) and index.
    ISBN 0-335-19872-4 (hardcover). — ISBN 0-335-19871-6 (pbk.)
    1. Imagination in children. 2. Creativity in children. 3. Early childhood education. I. Title. II. Series.
    LB1062.D84   1998
    370.15′7—dc21   97-39366
                                                             CIP

Typeset by Type Study, Scarborough

Printed and bound in Great Britain by
Marston Lindsay Ross International Ltd,
Oxfordshire

For Tricia

1965–95

'I am certain of nothing but the holiness of the heart's affections and the truth of imagination'

Keats, Letter to Benjamin Bailey,
22 November 1817

Contents

List of tables

Acknowledgements

I am grateful to the many children, parents and colleagues I have had the privilege to work with over the last twenty years, some of whom will recognize episodes in the book. Special thanks go to all those involved in the Dorothy Gardner Centre – they are an endless source of inspiration.

Vicky Hurst and Jenefer Joseph have shown great faith by asking me to write this, my first book. I hope that this faith is justified and thank them for the encouragement, help and support along the way. Anne Culliford, Deva Priya and Jane Lambert have acted as critical readers and spent many hours studying the text and offering suggestions, insights and reassurance. Thank you!

My nieces and nephews, Tom, Matty, Katie and Nancy feature through-out the book and I hope that in later years they approve! I am grateful to them and their parents, Angela, Jackie and both Pauls for allowing me to share and use these episodes from the early years of their life.

Finally, an award for patience goes to my husband Stan, who, over the final months, has given his whole-hearted support during frequent bouts of despair and frustration! He has offered encouragement and practical support (not least in proofreading the text) as well as providing a model of an individual who uses his creativity and imagination to the full. My love and thanks.

Series editors' preface

This book is one of a series which will be of interest to all those who are concerned with the care and education of children from birth to 6 years old – childminders, teachers and other professionals in schools, those who work in playgroups, private and community nurseries and similar institutions; governors, providers and managers. We also speak to parents and carers, whose involvement is probably the most influential of all for children's learning and development.

Our focus is on improving the effectiveness of early education. Policy developments come and go, and difficult decisions are often forced on all those with responsibility for young children's well-being. We aim to help with these decisions by showing how developmental approaches to young children's education not only accord with our fundamental educational principles, but provide a positive and sound basis for learning.

Each book recognizes and demonstrates that children from birth to 6 years old have particular developmental learning needs, and that all those providing care and education for them would be wise to approach their work developmentally. This applies just as much to the acquisition of subject knowledge, skills and understanding, as to other educational goals such as social skills, attitudes and dispositions. In this series there are several volumes with a subject-based focus, and the main aim is to show how that can be introduced to young children within the framework of an integrated and developmentally appropriate curriculum, without losing its integrity as an area of knowledge in its own right. We also stress the importance of providing a learning environment which is carefully planned for children's own active learning. This volume explores the exciting world which embraces all the Arts, shows its attractiveness to children almost from birth, and demonstrates its importance for the all-round development of human beings.

Access for all children is fundamental to the provision of educational opportunity. We are concerned to emphasize anti-discriminatory approaches throughout, as well as the importance of recognizing that meeting special educational needs must be an integral purpose of curriculum development and planning. We see the role of play in learning as a central one, and one which also relates to all-round emotional, social and physical development. Play, along with other forms of active learning, is normally a natural point of access to the curriculum for each child at his or her particular stage and level of understanding. It is therefore an essential force in making for equal opportunities in learning, intrinsic as it is to all areas of development. We believe that these two aspects, play and equal opportunities, are so important that we not only highlight them in each volume in this series, but also include separate volumes on them as well.

Throughout this series, we encourage readers to reflect on the education being offered to young children, through revisiting the developmental principles which most practitioners hold, and using them to analyse their observations of the children. In this way, readers can evaluate ideas about the most effective ways of educating young children, and develop strategies for approaching their practice in ways which exemplify their fundamental educational beliefs, and offer every child a more appropriate education.

The authors of each book in the series subscribe to the following set of principles for a developmental curriculum:

Principles for a developmental curriculum

- Each child is an individual and should be respected and treated as such.
- The early years are a period of development in their own right, and education of young children should be seen as a specialism with its own valid criteria of appropriate practice.
- The role of the educator of young children is to engage actively with what most concerns the child, and to support learning through these preoccupations.
- The educator has a responsibility to foster positive attitudes in children to both self and others, and to counter negative messages which children may have received.

- Each child's cultural and linguistic endowment is seen as the fundamental medium of learning.
- An anti-discriminatory approach is the basis of all respect-worthy education, and is essential as a criterion for a developmentally appropriate curriculum (DAC).
- All children should be offered equal opportunities to progress and develop, and should have equal access to good quality provision. The concepts of multiculturalism and anti-racism are intrinsic to this whole educational approach.
- Partnership with parents should be given priority as the most effective means of ensuring coherence and continuity in children's experiences, and in the curriculum offered to them.
- A democratic perspective permeates education of good quality and is the basis of transactions between people.

Vicky Hurst and Jenefer Joseph

Introduction

Example

James, aged 6 and Daniel, aged 4, are parading slowly round the table. At the table sit their parents, grandparents, aunt and uncle finishing a meal and arguing the relative musical merits of Mozart, Dire Straits and Deep Purple. James leads and explains to Daniel 'We're climbing the Himalayas, to find Baby Jesus, it's a dangerous journey.' Round and round the table they go, James miming climbing a rope and Daniel copying him. As they go Daniel serves tea using a toy tea set to the adults at the table who pretend to drink and ask how the journey is progressing. Suddenly, James stops, 'We're at the top, look there's Baby Jesus !' Daniel runs to get a toy panda 'This is Baby Jesus!'

What are James and Daniel doing? They are obviously not in the Himalayas and Daniel's panda is not Baby Jesus! The adults with them do not find this behaviour strange; quite the reverse. They join in the pretence when asked and support it through questions about the boys' progress up the pretend mountain to find Baby Jesus. It would appear that in this family, as in many others, the use of the imagination to create a pretend situation is fostered and appreciated.

In the following chapters I will argue that creativity and imagination are vital to development and that they have an important function in early childhood and throughout life. I will seek to explain why the sort of behaviour exhibited by James and Daniel, and countless other children we know and care for, should be valued and encouraged. I will assert that creativity and imagination should be a central focus of their education.

This book is part of the 'Supporting Early Learning Series' and while creativity and imagination are part of the process of learning across all curriculum areas, it will concentrate on their development through:

- two- and three-dimensional representations
- music
- dance
- imaginative play

as these are the learning experiences that are most often put under a label of creative development. Through these experiences children express their feelings, thoughts and responses. Such experiences stimulate open-ended activity which encourages discovery, exploration, experimentation and invention. All these skills are vital to creativity and imagination.

There is a growing awareness of the abilities and potential of young children. The right of young children to maintain and develop these abilities and potentials is now recognized. 'Every child has the right to rest and leisure, to engage in play and recreational activities appropriate to the age of the child and to participate freely in cultural life and the arts' (Article 31 of the United Nations Rights of the Child).

Table I shows how the learning experiences described in this book relate to the requirements of:

1 Desirable Outcomes for Children's Learning on Entry to Compulsory Schooling – School Curriculum and Assessment Authority.
2 National Curriculum – Department of Education and Employment.
3 National Vocational Qualifications – Council for Awards in Child Care and Education.

I have drawn on my experience of promoting young children's creativity and imagination in a variety of settings over the last twenty years. The settings include home-based and centre-based care, and this book draws on the practical experience of adults living and working with young children in these settings. Many of the examples are from the experiences of staff, parents and children at the Dorothy Gardner Centre, a combined nursery centre in a culturally and linguistically rich area of London.

My aim has been to use real-life examples of young children's development and their growing competence to show the richness of their creativity and imagination. I have drawn on research findings to inform

Table I The links between this book and . . .

Desirable Outcomes – School Curriculum and Assessment Council 1996	National Curriculum – Department for Education 1995	National Vocational Qualifications – Council for Awards in Child Care and Education 1991	Supporting creativity and imagination in the early years
Heading: Creative Development	*Heading:* Art in the National Curriculum Music in the National Curriculum Physical Education in the National Curriculum – Dance	*Heading:* Set out natural and other materials for creative play level II Help children to express their imagination and creativity level III	*Heading:* Creativity and imagination
Includes: Art Music Dance Imaginative play Stories	*Includes:* Art • investigating and making • knowledge and understanding Music • performing and composing • listening and appraising Dance	*Includes:* Creative art / craft activities Music / rhythmical activities Dance / drama Role / fantasy play Stories / written work Water / sand	*Includes:* Art Music Dance Imaginative play

everyday practice and have restricted academic or professional jargon to a minimum. Examples of good practice are highlighted in boxes and each chapter ends with a summary, suggestions for further reading and 'things to think about'.

This book is for all those who delight in young children's learning and development and want to explore new ways of supporting it. I hope that it will help readers to reflect on principles and practice, challenge assumptions and encourage discussion.

Bernadette Duffy
The Dorothy Gardner Centre

Part One

What are creativity and imagination and why are they important?

The future belongs to those who do not rein in their imagination

Chukovsky (1963: 122)

The importance of creativity and imagination for society and young children

Introduction

This chapter will examine the:

- importance of creativity and imagination for society
- need to respond to a rapidly changing world
- dangers of undervaluing creativity and imagination
- importance of visual literacy
- importance of creativity and imagination for children
- contribution of creativity and imagination to other areas of learning.

Creativity and imagination

Creativity and imagination are much used words and it would appear that we think that what they represent is, generally, a good thing. In recent months I have been urged to be creative with soya and net curtains by magazines, and television presenters have instructed me on how to be imaginative with my window boxes. At a recent conference a speaker promised to explain the creative approach to base-line assessment and a radio commentator decried the lack of imagination displayed by players during a football match. The only negative comment has been the note my tutor wrote on a returned assignment despairing of my creative spelling!

For Cecil et al. (1985) creativity is an indicator of quality in early childhood settings and a high degree of mental health in the individual. We are urged to promote creativity and imaginative qualities by:

- Her Majesty's Inspectorate 1989: Teaching should encourage children 'to be imaginative and creative' (*Aspects of Primary Education: The Education of Children Under Five*, p. 8).
- The School Curriculum and Assessment Authority 1996: Settings must ensure 'the development of children's imagination and their ability to communicate and to express ideas in creative ways' (*Desirable Outcomes for Children's Learning on Entry to Compulsory Education*, p. 4).
- The Department for Education 1995: 'Pupils should be taught the creative, imaginative and practical skills they need to express ideas and feelings, record observation, design and make images and artifacts' (*Art Programme of Study in the National Curriculum*, p. 2).
- National Vocational Qualifications in Child Care and Education 1991: Candidates must know how to 'Set out natural and other materials for creative play' and 'Help children to express their imagination and creativity' (*Council for Awards in Child Care and Education*, pp. C8.2 and C10.8).

This emphasis on the importance of creativity and imagination is not new. Froebel in the nineteenth century associated creativity and imagination with the inner life of the child. 'We become truly Godlike in diligence and industry, in working and doing, which are accompanied by the clear perception or even the vaguest feeling that thereby we represent the inner in the outer' (Froebel 1826: 31). Creativity and imagination are seen as good things and have a long tradition in early childhood settings. But why are they important?

The importance of creativity and imagination for society

The human desire to be creative has been present throughout history in all communities. Creation myths devised by religious and cultural groups reflect this desire. A number of these use the imagery of human creativity to express divine creativity. The clay of the potter is used as the raw material of creation – the Creator moulds and sculpts the clay to create human beings. For example, the Chinese story of creation describes how Numa, the mother goddess, created people from the river mud to ease her loneliness. Jewish, Christian, and Islamic traditions describe God creating man and woman from the dust of the ground. In Greek mythology Prometheus uses the clay to make little images of the gods (Lynch 1992). The myths emphasize the desire to create, the pleasure in the creation and the sense of ownership towards the created. These emotions are reflected in our own experience of creativity. The sense of pleasure and satisfaction derived from the creative process is part of all our experience, whether this is finding a solution to a problem, preparing a special meal, writing an assignment which has stretched our understanding or composing a piece of music.

As we can see from the existence of prehistoric cave paintings, from earliest times human beings have made their mark using the materials available to them. The desire to represent and share our experiences with others, for example through art, music and dance, seems to be a basic human characteristic. Trevarthen argues that we are born with this need to share and understand the ideas, thoughts and feelings of others and from this need the representations of our culture, such as the visual and performing arts, have developed (Trevarthen 1995).

We have all been touched by a powerful experience of beauty in the visual or performing arts, maybe in our response to a beautiful painting or a piece of music and again the myths human beings have created reflect this. For example, there is a Hindu story which tells of the God Vishnu turning himself into a dancing girl to stop the demons from gaining the nectar of life. The beauty of the dance absorbs the demons and allows the gods to gain the nectar. As human beings we need to exercise our creativity and imagination, we need to represent our thoughts, impressions and feelings.

We are all users of artifacts and ideas that are the result of creative thought, for example through the clothes we wear and the technology we use. Most of us are also makers who rely, in some way, on our creativity and imagination. Maybe as artists or artisans or in everyday situations, such as in the arrangement of our living spaces to produce a pleasing environment. Society has always needed people who are creative and imaginative, people who are able to come up with creative solutions to problems and imaginatively combine previously unconnected ideas and skills.

Creative and imaginative experiences give us the opportunity to:

- develop the full range of human potential
- improve our capacity for thought, action and communication
- nurture our feelings and sensibilities
- extend our physical and perceptual skills
- explore values
- understand our own and other cultures.

(Calouste Gulbenkian 1982)

The need to respond to a rapidly changing world

The world we live in is changing rapidly and the pace of change has never been faster. We do not know the challenges that will face the children we work with in their adult lives but we do know that in order to meet these challenges they will need to be creative and imaginative. Today's children will need to grow into adults who can:

- deal with the unexpected
- extend current knowledge to new situations
- bring together previously unconnected information
- use information in a new way
- experiment with novel concepts
- deal with incessant change
- be able to reappraise values and ways of working
- modify and monitor their world
- think flexibly
- play with ideas and materials
- work with people from a diversity of cultures, language and religions
- empathize with others
- collaborate in various ways with different people
- take risks
- be innovative
- respond imaginatively to challenges.

Unfortunately, we have often undervalued the creative and imaginative ways of thinking that encourage these characteristics.

The undervaluing of creativity and imagination

Bruner (1986) has argued that we have placed great value on logical and systematic thought and intuitive thought has not received the attention it deserves. This has led to an over-emphasis on the ability to retain and repeat facts, to be impartial, dispassionate and detached. It can mean that learning is not through first-hand experiences, but is based on accepting the understandings of others with the result that our ability to see the world through our own eyes decreases. When only the rational aspects of learning and development are stressed we deprive ourselves of the full range of the human ability to think.

The growth of scientific and technological ways of knowing has been associated with undervaluing the creative and imaginative ways. But we do this at our peril. As Heckscher explains, 'in every great discovery there has always been somewhere along the line a creative act, a leap of imagination' (Heckscher 1966: 98). Understanding science and technology requires the ability to think creatively as much as any of the arts subjects traditionally associated with this aspect of learning. For example, Newton's discovery of gravity involved a creative jump from the observed event of the apple falling to the theory of gravity – an immense generalization. Zohar and Marshall (1997) see the divide between science and the arts as unnatural and are seeking to redress the imbalance. Today's scientists often employ the vocabulary of aesthetics in describing their work. It is not unusual for a theory to be described as 'beautiful' or 'elegant'.

There should be no conflict between the two modes of thinking, between the logical and the intuitive. It is not a case of either/or but of both. They offer complementary views, and when combined, advance our understanding of the world in which we live and our ability to respond creatively to the challenges it presents.

The importance of visual literacy

In communities where creativity and imagination are championed, visual literacy is promoted. Visual literacy involves the ability to identify and describe what we see and evaluate its aesthetic qualities and fitness for purpose. For example, when looking at a painting, sculpture or textile, we may consider the visual effect the artist was trying to create and decide whether the materials and methods used have achieved this. When assessing the man-made environment we may consider the materials used and the way in which they are arranged. Is the effect pleasing to the eye? Are they the right materials for the purpose for which they were intended, for example, does the roof leak?

The urban sprawl that blights many areas is a direct result of the lack of visual literacy in many of our communities (Pickering 1976). Drab surroundings and poorly made products frustrate and depress us. As a society, we are visually illiterate and not well versed in the appreciation of beauty. We need to learn how to see and:

- be able to look critically with knowledge and understanding of, for example, aesthetic values, design, construction
- have the vocabulary to describe and comment on what we see. For example, the elements of art – line, tone, texture, pattern, colour, shape, form, space
- have the desire to promote and produce an aesthetically pleasing environment.

Visual literacy is everyone's entitlement. The Art Programme of study in the National Curriculum recognizes this right. 'In order to develop literacy, pupils should be taught about the different ways in which ideas, feelings and meanings are communicated in visual form' (DfE 1995: 2). Adults who lack insight and the ability to understand the perceptual world, who are illiterate and inadequate in one of the most fundamental domains of human experience, have been denied their entitlement (Pickering 1976).

The importance of creativity and imagination for the child

It is not only for the sake of future society that we need to educate young children in ways that emphasize and encourage their imagination and creativity but for the here and now. As stated in the Preface to this series, education in the early years is valid in its own right. By encouraging creativity and imagination we are promoting children's ability to explore and comprehend their world and increasing their opportunities to make new connections and reach new understandings. Young children are naturally curious about the people and world around them and they want to know more about their relationship to them. Through their imagination children can move from the present into the past and the future, to what might be and beyond. They are freed from the world of immediate sensations. Through their creative and imaginative endeavours children:

- communicate their feelings in non-verbal and pre-verbal ways, for example, using gestures, movement and dance
- express their thoughts, for example, by painting and drawing
- comprehend, respond and represent their perceptions and understanding of the world, for example, by the roles they adopt in their imaginative play
- experience beauty and lasting value
- express their cultural heritage and increase their understanding of other cultures
- think about and create new meanings
- solve problems and gain mastery
- gain self-esteem, for instance, by celebrating their identity (see Figure 1.1).

They can create an image and view of the world that is uniquely their own. By examining children's creative and imaginative expressions we can find out what they know about their world, what they consider important and how they choose to represent it.

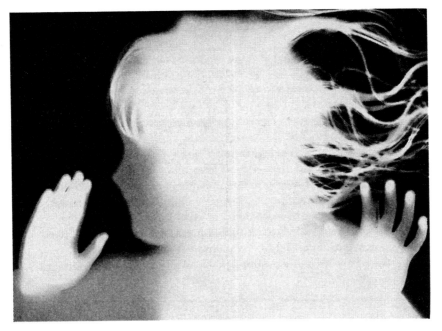

Figure 1.1   Carla, aged 4 years 6 months, created this self-portrait by lying on a sheet of photographic paper which was then exposed to light.

The importance of representation

Children need to represent their experiences, their feelings and ideas if they are to preserve them and share them with others. When we represent we make an object or symbol stand for something else, for example, we may use our imagination to pretend that the toy doll is a real baby or draw a picture that symbolizes our experience of going to the zoo. Spoken language is also a form of symbolic representation, words standing for something in the real world. Matthews (1994) stresses the significance of children acquiring this ability. From it springs the understanding to comprehend other forms of symbolic representation, such as written language and mathematics. Representation has a central role in cognitive development and it is through symbolic representation that children acquire the facility for abstract thought.

Once children can separate objects and actions from their meaning in the real world and give them new meanings they are no longer tied to the concrete world and start to think in an abstract way. For example, if they can pretend that a stick is no longer a stick but is to be used as if it were a

---

Example

Many years ago I decided that the reception class children I worked
with would create a picture to represent Spring. I carefully cut out hills
for the background and showed the children how to represent grass
using sponge printing. I decided to use egg boxes to create flowers and
explained to the children how to cut them to make daffodils and
crocuses. Bulrushes and lambs were made using painted cotton wool. I
was pleased with the finished result. The children showed less
enthusiasm. They had worked hard to produce the display but the end
result had little relevance to them. The inner city area in which the
school was situated did not feature green hills, lambs or bulrushes!
The children had not been involved in discussing the images that
represented spring for them or how to produce these images. It was
not an example of the children's creativity but of mine.

Creativity is about representing one's own image, not reproducing
someone else's.

---

hairbrush, they can start to understand that the marks 'c a t' on a page,
which do not look or sound like a cat, can be used to represent a cat.

Children represent their experiences in a number of ways. They may:

- draw a picture
- describe an experience in words
- use role play to act out a situation
- build a model using blocks
- use movement and dance to express an emotion
- paint a picture
- compose a piece of music.

Children use their representations to explore, to solve problems, to think
about and create new meanings. Different forms of representation enable
them to address problems in various ways and gain new insights. The
ability and opportunity to represent offers children a sense of control
which enhances their self-image.

Too often activities that are labelled as creative in schools, nurseries and
at home are about filling time, learning a set of techniques or decoration
rather than being truly creative, intellectual activities. Pre-printed, adult-
directed and mass-produced art work does not lead to creativity. The
images that the children create using these methods are not their own.
Such work may occupy children and fill empty walls. It may look pretty
and be admired, but it will not encourage imagination and creativity.

McKellar (1957) is clear about the difference between reproduction and creativity. When we are engaged in reproduction we use a single source of information and the result is predictable. When we are being creative we use information from a variety of sources which are fused together to produce an integrated whole. These sources may include images that other people have created but this is combined with information from other sources, including our imagination. Simply copying the image of another is reproduction not creativity.

Children are surrounded by ready-made images and will naturally assimilate and draw on the images of their culture (Matthews 1994). For example, many 1-year-olds recognize the sign for the McDonald's hamburger chain or the bus stop, and early drawings of houses often owe more to traditional images of houses they have seen than to the realities of the child's own home. Part of our role is to ensure that the children have the opportunity to explore a range of representations both from their own and other cultures and times. But children must also have the opportunity to go beyond this, to produce their own representations that reflect their own experiences, thoughts and feelings.

The contributions creativity and imagination make to other areas of learning

Translating ideas, concepts and experiences into representations involves many thinking skills. Creativity and imagination are important in their own right and also because they foster the development of the whole child by promoting learning across the curriculum. Table 1.1 shows some of the contributions that the creative and imaginative areas of experience can make to other areas of learning. The table uses a combination of the headings adopted by Desirable Outcomes for Learning (DfEE 1996) and the National Curriculum.

Conclusion

If we want adults who are creative and imaginative we must start in their earliest years. We are educating children for life and the attitudes that we promote at this stage will remain with them. If we do not promote creativity and imagination, children will not become the people we need them to be.

It is important to take a long-term view. Preparing children only for the short term, whether this is the next test or the next stage in their education

Table 1.1 Some of the contributions creativity and imagination make to other areas of learning

Personal and social	Language and literacy	Mathematics
• concentration, staying on task, problem-solving, planning and seeing things through to completion • representing experiences, feelings and thoughts, for example, by using drawings, painting and imaginative play • learning to learn to share, interact and observe others, for instance, through working together on joint projects *Spiritual and moral* • a creative process that links children with the idea of creation in world religions • exposure to the arts through which children learn about their own and other cultures • a sense of self-respect and valuing of others, for example, through appraising	Speaking and listening • opportunities to speak and listen, for example, when negotiating roles and sharing resources • understanding the elements of music, such as rhythm and pitch, from which develops children's ability to speak *Reading* • understanding the process of representation which leads to understanding the symbolic nature of written language *Writing* • the fine motor skills which are needed for writing, for example, through drawing or using woodwork tools • the narrative skills necessary for story-telling, for example, by engaging in imaginative play	• understanding patterns in two- and three-dimensional representations which helps children to identify number patterns later on • concepts of shape, size, line and area which they will use to classify and sort objects • the opportunity to explore spatial concepts for example through block play and other forms of three-dimensional representation • the opportunity to explore measurement in meaning full contexts while constructing models and textiles • symbolic representation which introduces children to the concepts they will need to record data

Table 1.1 Continued

Knowledge and understanding of the world		Physical

Science/technology
- exposure to a wide range of materials and their properties, for example, through using a wide range of methods for fastening – sticking, tying, nailing – discovering the most appropriate method for a particular task
- cause and effect, for instance, through experimenting with different ways of balancing blocks
- representations based on observations of the natural world which develop an understanding of life and living process
- opportunities to cut, fold and fasten
- problem-solving, for example, deciding best media to use to create a representation

History/geography
- opportunities to reflect on what children know about their locality and the wider world, for instance, through representing their local environment using a variety of media
- sequencing events and objects, for example, when creating a pattern on a piece of clay
- expressing views on attractive and unattractive features of the environment
- exposure to artifacts, dance and music from a variety of cultures and times which helps children to develop a sense of time and place
- representation and a sense of spatial awareness which is needed in map-making
- making up stories about the past and factual accounts

Physical
- opportunities to develop and practise fine motor skills, for example, through cutting, drawing, sculpting, playing an instrument
- gross motor skills, for instance, through dance and block play
- planning, performing and practising physical skills
- linking actions and work with others, for example, through dancing together and working on large construction
- exposure to dance traditions
- exploring mood and feeling using movement
- body control, balance, coordination and poise

is short-sighted. We are in the business of preparing children for a future that we can only imagine. The need to measure and test can lead to a narrowing of the curriculum and a concentration on the logical and systematic ways of thinking we looked at earlier. If we teach only what is easy to measure and test we will lose much that is valuable. At a time when there is an emphasis on the basic skills of literacy and numeracy it is crucial to remind ourselves of the importance of creativity and imagination in their own right and in the contribution they make to other areas of learning. We need to resist any attempt to curtail or limit the development of creativity and imagination in the early years and beyond. If we do not ensure plenty of opportunities for learning that are first hand; that encourage children to think for themselves; to play and to take risks, we will raise a generation who, to quote Oscar Wilde, 'know the price of everything and the value of nothing' (Wilde 1969 *Lady Windermere's Fan*, Act III).

Through a curriculum rich in creative and imaginative opportunities young children have the opportunity to develop skills, attitudes and knowledge that will benefit all areas of their learning and development. If our wishes for the children are to become reality we must plan provision for young children that encourages and develops creativity and imagination. We need to find ways of promoting what we value and making our beliefs real.

Creativity and imagination come from the human ability to play and civilization rests on this ability. It is essential that we foster the human capacity for creativity and play, if we do not we will be left copying old ideas. Involvement in creative and imaginative experiences should be for life.

Summary

This chapter has:

- outlined the importance of creativity and imagination for society and young children
- identified the dangers of undervaluing creativity and imagination
- stressed the importance of visual literacy
- looked at the importance of representation
- shown the contribution creativity and imagination make to all areas of learning.

Further reading

Matthews, J. (1994) *Helping Children to Draw and Paint in Early Childhood*. London: Hodder and Stoughton.
Matthews looks at the development and importance of graphic representation.
McKellar, P. (1957) *Imagination and Thinking: A Psychological Analysis*. London: Cohen and West.
A study of the interaction of reason and the imagination.
Pickering, J. (1976) 'Visual education for young children', in D. Brothwell (ed.), *Beyond Aesthetics: Investigating into the Nature of Visual Art*. London: Thames and Hudson.
Pickering offers a justification for visual education.
Trevarthen, C. (1995) The child's need to learn a culture. *Children and Society*, 9, 1: 5–19.
Trevarthen argues that babies are highly motivated to learn about their culture.

Things to think about

- How do you express creativity and imagination in your own life?

- Could you explain the importance of creativity and imagination to someone else?

- Is there agreement between yourself and those you live and work with about the importance of creativity and imagination?

- How do you encourage creativity and imagination in your work with young children?

Defining creativity and imagination

Introduction

This chapter will:

- look at definitions of creativity and imagination
- look at the link between creativity and imagination
- look at the characteristics of creativity in young children
- identify the links with aesthetics and art
- identify the links with play.

Definitions of creativity and imagination

The experiences we offer children in their earliest years are crucial in their future development. The richer these early experiences are, the more opportunity children will have to develop the dispositions and understandings that they need now and in the future. But defining creativity and imagination can be difficult. Definitions may:

- limit creativity and imagination to the production of an artifact, for example, a painting
- restrict creativity and imagination to the 'arts', as being only to do with painting or music

- see them simply as a skill – something which can be taught by means of instruction
- view them as something that will develop if the conditions are right
- include stereotypical concepts, for example, that certain groups of people are naturally creative
- limit creativity and imagination to the gifted few.

We need to develop definitions of creativity and imagination that:

- are not elitist
- recognize that all children have the ability to be creative and imaginative
- makes the most of the talents of all children
- embrace the idea that all children need opportunities to play with ideas
- acknowledge the importance of an environment which encourages and values creativity and imagination.

Creativity and imagination are often linked, for instance in *Desirable Outcomes for Children's Learning on Entry to Compulsory Education* (DfEE 1996), but they are not interchangeable. If we are to promote them effectively we need to be clear about what they are and how they relate to each other. We also need to be clear about their links with areas such as aesthetics and play.

On the following pages are a number of definitions of creativity and imagination. The definitions are taken from a variety of sources. Some are well-known researchers and educationalists, others are simply people I stopped and asked at random! Each of their definitions is slightly different and reflects their experience and area of expertise. For example, Robert's definition sees creativity as intrinsic to humanity. This reflects his life as a musician and composer. He is continually striving to be creative and therefore defines it as part of human nature.

Creativity is:

> 'a thinking and responding process that involves connecting with our previous experience, responding to stimuli (objects, symbols, ideas, people, situations) and generally at least one unique combination.'
>
> Parnes (1963: 5)

'to create – to bring into existence.'
  Oxford English Dictionary

'the expression of original ideas, an intrinsic part of humanity.'
Robert – Musician and composer

'the ability to make what you picture exist.'
Francis – Gardener

'producing something with inspiration.'
Caroline – Mother of three

'being clever and designing.'
James – aged 6

'to dare to be different.'
Claxton (1984: 228)

'the ability or capacity to mentally or physically construct or reconstruct reality in a unique way.'
Theresa – Educational facilitator

'the impetus for learning.'
John – Early years educator

'to fulfil our potential.'
Elizabeth – Early education lecturer

Creativity

These definitions show that creativity involves:

- the ability to see things in fresh ways
- learning from past experiences and relating this learning to new situations
- thinking along unorthodox lines and breaking barriers
- using non-traditional approaches to solving problems
- going further than the information given
- creating something unique or original.

McKellar (1957) states that all creative thought has external sources which may be remote or recent, conscious or unconscious. Creativity does not occur in a vacuum. The creative element is in connecting and re-arranging information from these sources.
To do this we need:

- the necessary skills and abilities to realize our ideas
- a body of knowledge and understanding to explore and find new combinations
- the attitudes and dispositions that enable us to continue with a task until our ideas are realized.

For me, creativity means connecting the previously unconnected in ways that are new and meaningful to the individual concerned.

Imagination is:

'play without action.'
Vygotsky (1978: 43)

'the ability to conjure up visual, tactile, or aural images in one's mind.'
Robert – Musician and composer

'the ability to picture what doesn't exist.'
Francis – Gardener

'imagination – a mental faculty for forming images not yet present.'
Oxford English Dictionary

'seeing what isn't there, Daniel thinking there's a ghost in the wardrobe.'
James – aged 6

'the ability to form rich and varied mental images or concepts of people, places, things, situations not present.'
Isenberg and Jalongo (1993: 7)

'a cognitive capacity to picture in one's mind an alternative reality.'
Theresa – Educational facilitator

'imagination – fancy, inspiration, vision . . .'
Roget's Thesaurus, 1985

'what makes us human.'
Jo – Nursery teacher

Imagination

The definitions demonstrate some of the elements that are part of imagination. To imagine is to:

- detach oneself from the tangible world and move beyond concrete situations
- not be restricted to the immediate perceived world
- internalize perceptions
- separate action and objects from their meaning in the real world and give them new meanings
- bring together and integrate experiences and perceptions
- contemplate what is not but might be; to pretend.

The way in which our perceptions are turned into images, stored and used, will depend on the individual. Different people appear to have a preference for particular images and the ability to imagine varies between individuals (McKellar 1957). For example, when we imagine we may draw on:

- visual experiences – what we have seen
- aural experiences   – what we have heard
- tactile experiences – what we have felt.

Fantasy is a form of imagination where what is imagined has little resemblance to the real world. If imagination is defined as the ability to think 'as if', fantasy is the ability to think 'what if' (Weininger 1988). For me, imagination is internalizing our perceptions, and using them and objects to create meanings that do not depend on the external world.

The links between creativity and imagination

As we can see from the definitions we have looked at, creativity and imagination, while they are not the same thing, are clearly connected. Creativity frequently involves the use of the imagination. For example:

- Velcro, which makes clothing so easy to fasten, was created as the result of its inventor's observation that burrs caught on his clothing as he crossed a field. He examined the burrs closely and noticed the tiny hooks that attached themselves to his clothing. From this observation he used his imagination to envisage the model for a fastener. Many people over the years had noticed this capacity in burrs but he was the first to see the wider application. He used his creativity to connect his observation of the burrs to the needs of clothing.
- In order to engage in work on population genetics, scientists utilize imaginary numbers. The square root of minus one does not exist in real life but is crucial to formulas used in this field. Without this imagined number, problems in population genetics would not have been solved and thinking would not have progressed.

When we are making new connections we often use our ability to imagine in order to detach ourselves from the immediate world, internalize our perceptions and explore a range of possibilities. But we are not always being creative when we are using our imagination. For example, children's imaginative play can be repetitive, they may simply be repeating well-known roles and scenarios. The definitions of imagination and creativity given by the gardener, Francis can help us to see the difference – while imagination is the ability to picture what does not exist, the creative element is in turning what we imagine into reality. Or, as Froebel puts it, when we are being creative 'we give body to thought . . . we render visible the invisible' (Froebel 1826: 31).

The characteristics of creativity in young children

A number of the definitions of creativity and imagination we have used so far focus on the discovery of the new, of connecting the previously unconnected, and the ability to internalize our perceptions using our imagination. How do we relate these definitions to young children? Most of the things they discover are not new, but have been discovered by others long before. However, these discoveries are new to the child. We define creativity in children as being when, for the first time, they make a connection that they have not previously made. Isenberg and Jalongo (1993) offer these ways of defining creativity in the early years. Children are being creative when they:

- explore and experiment
- use language and play to make sense of the world
- concentrate on a single task for a long period
- bring order out of chaos and do something new with the old and familiar
- use repetition to learn something new (see Figure 2.1).

Links with aesthetics and art

Creativity and imagination are often linked with aesthetics. For example, *Aspects of Primary Education: The Education of Children Under Five* produced

---

Example

Genise, aged 4 years and 5 months, visited Richmond Park with her key worker group. This was her first visit to the park and what interested her most were the deer. The antlers were especially fascinating. Genise commented 'they're like trees!' She gathered twigs to take back to the Nursery Centre and attached them to a band of card to make her own set of antlers. Genise found her own way to create antlers. She had not seen anyone else make antlers before but connected the shape of the antlers she observed to her knowledge of trees and twigs. She used her knowledge of hat-making to create a band to attach the antlers to.

Figure 2.1 Young children are being creative when they explore and experiment, use play to make sense of the world, concentrate on a single task for a long time and do something new with the old and familiar. Adam, aged 2 years 3 months, spent two hours creating his own representation of an airport using blocks.

by Her Majesty's Inspectorate in 1989 describes the aesthetic and creative area of learning as 'central to children's learning' (HMI 1989: 29). Aesthetics is the investigation of beauty in colour, form and design. It includes responding to and taking pleasure from what is considered beautiful, whether in art, dance, music or life.

Creativity and imagination are linked with art in Article 31 of the United Nations Convention on Human Rights which defines art as 'the whole range of creative and imaginative self-expression undertaken by people of all cultures, classes and ages'.

In the National Curriculum creativity and imagination are also seen as part of art, and as a component of the programme of study children should be taught to 'express ideas and feelings, record observations, design and make images and artifacts' (DfE 1995: 2.)

The links with play

There are many links and overlaps between the creative process and play. Play and creativity share many of the same characteristics – indeed play is often seen as part of the creative process. They both involve:

- an attitude *and* a process
- a state of mind and disposition
- the ability to cope with uncertainty
- the ability to explore new ideas
- divergent thinking, which is the ability to look at a problem in a variety of ways
- a lack of constraint
- the existence of choice
- creating and re-creating.

Imagination and creativity are firmly rooted within play (Moyles 1989) and playfulness remains part of the creative process throughout life. Play promotes the flexibility and problem-solving skills that are needed to be creative. Artists will often talk about playing with materials to discover new, creative combinations. By continuing to be playful as adults, by consciously using the characteristics of play, we are able to gain information through all the senses rather than being limited to second-hand information or predetermined outcomes. An attitude of playfulness enables imaginative possibilities to remain and imaginative leaps to take place (Prentice 1994).

Conclusion

In this chapter I have offered a variety of definitions, but the definitions I will use in this book are: *creativity* is about connecting the previously unconnected in ways that are new and meaningful to the individual; *imagination* is about internalizing perceptions and ascribing objects and events with new meanings. Creativity and imagination may be hard to define but they are part of what makes us uniquely human.

Summary

In this chapter I have:

- offered a number of definitions of creativity and imagination

- established a working definition of creativity and imagination
- argued that creativity and imagination are a state of mind and disposition
- stressed that creativity and imagination are part of a process
- emphasized the link between creativity and play.

Further reading

Isenberg, J.P. and Jalongo, M.R. (1993) *Creative Expression and Play in the Early Childhood Curriculum.* Englewood-Cliffs, New Jersey: Prentice-Hall.
Chapter 1 offers definitions of creativity and discusses creativity in young children.
McKellar, J. (1957) *Imagination and Thinking: A Psychological Analysis.* London: Cohen and West.
Chapter 1 looks at imagination, thinking and the dream. Chapter 2 examines mental imagery.
Moyles, J. (1989) *Just Playing?* Buckingham: Open University Press.
Chapter 5 deals with the links between play and creativity.

Things to think about

- Are you clear about the attributes of creativity and imagination?
- Consider the definitions of creativity and imagination. Do you agree with them?
- How would you define creativity and imagination?
- How are creativity and imagination demonstrated by young children?
- Do those you work and live with share your views?

3

Creative and imaginative experiences

Introduction

This chapter will look at:

- the dangers of a narrow approach
- the importance of access to a wide range of experiences
- the importance of access for all
- valuing children's race, religion, culture, class and ethnicity
- valuing children's gender
- valuing children with special educational needs
- two-dimensional experiences and the possibilities for learning they offer
- three-dimensional experiences and the possibilities for learning they offer
- musical experiences and the possibilities for learning they offer
- dance experiences and the possibilities for learning they offer
- imaginative play experiences and the possibilities for learning they offer
- experiences which encourage appraising and appreciating
- the need for depth of experience
- the need for differentiation.

The dangers of a narrow approach

Too often young children are given access to a narrow range of creative and imaginative experiences which are limited and superficial. For example, opportunities to paint can be restricted to using a small number of ready mixed paints, with no choice of brush or paper texture, size or shape. As a 6-year-old boy told me, 'I like painting best *but* you can only paint at "choosing time". Miss says only one person at a time, no paint on the floor, don't mix the paints, one picture each so every one gets a turn *and* only if you've finished *all* your work. *I* don't think that's fair.' These sort of conditions lead to impoverished provision and depressed thinking. If children are to become competent and use the media for their own ends they need the opportunity and time to explore a wide range of experiences.

The importance of access to a wide range of experiences

Tables 3.1–3.5 outline the different experiences that are part of the creative and imaginative area of learning. Each experience offers possibilities for learning and if we are not aware of these we may miss opportunities and impede children's progress. We need to ensure that the creative and imaginative experiences we offer are:

- *broad*: they must include the full range of experiences
- *balanced*: they must not concentrate on one area of experience and restrict or neglect the rest
- *accessible*: children's access should be monitored and their learning and development systematically assessed.

While some of the experiences described in Tables 3.1–3.5 will be available all the time and provide our core provision, others may be introduced for a limited period in response to children's interest and needs. By giving children access to a variety of experiences we offer them the opportunity to learn and develop:

- attitudes, feelings and dispositions
- knowledge and understandings
- skills and abilities.

and to use these in their own creative and imaginative ways. Each of these features of learning is important. For example, there is little point in teaching children the technical skills involved in drawing or music if they do not also have the desire to use these skills to create their own drawings or music, or to understand the work of others. Conversely, it is frustrating to have a burning desire to create a sound but to lack the technical skills necessary to achieve it. While knowledge and skills can be taught, attitudes and feelings cannot be learnt through direct instruction, but only develop in an environment that is encouraging and values these attributes. Creative and imaginative experiences encourage a wide range of:

ATTITUDES, DISPOSITIONS, FEELINGS

fun   appreciation   confidence   self-motivation   values

enthusiasm   experimentation   persistence   sharing

curiosity   perseverance   enjoyment   cooperation

willingness   acceptance   excitement   reflection   self-esteem

concern   self-discipline   evaluation   concentration

helpfulness   pleasure   lack of inhibition   respect for others

---

As adults we divide reative and imaginative experiences into the different forms of representation, for example, painting, drawing, imaginative play, and into knowledge, skill and attitudes to help us to plan and monitor children's access to a broad and balanced range of experiences. Children will not divide or perceive the experiences on offer in this way. For them, experiences are not compartmentalized and attitudes, knowledge and skills do not develop in isolation from each other.

Access for all

As we established in Chapter 1, access to creative and imaginative experiences are not only for those identified as gifted. Everyone has an entitlement to the full range of experience and to reach their full potential – the principles which underpin this series of books reinforce this message. But the society we live in assigns different value to different groups of people based on their:

- race, religion, culture, class and ethnicity
- gender
- special educational needs.

People in particular groups are seen as inferior, for example, people whose skin is not white, people who have certain medical conditions (HIV positive, mental illness), or people who come from particular religions (Muslims, Jews). Children who belong to families in these groups can find that their access to the creative and imaginative experiences they need is limited because of beliefs based on the view that they are inferior.

Children from some groups appear to display marked ability in certain aspects of creativity and imagination. However, we need to be cautious about ascribing this to innate ability. It is just as likely to be the result of upbringing and expectations. For example:

- Some groups of Chinese children have highly developed drawing skills at an early age due to the value placed on and early instruction in these skills by the communities in which they live (Cox 1992).
- Boys often appear to be better than girls at creating three-dimensional representations with construction materials. While this may be partly the result of innate differences, most of the difference is due to the greater encouragement boys receive (Moyles 1989).

Children are aware of the values and judgements of the adults around them from a young age (DHSS 1989, *The Children Act: Guidance and Regulations*, Volume 2: 34). The distorted opinions that develop from exposure to beliefs that are based on prejudice and discrimination will stay with

---

Example

Leeanne, aged 5 years, was involved in acting out the story of Cinderella. This had gone on over a number of days and with each re-telling the narrative became more complex and detailed. She reached the point in her drama when she needed the ballgown. With the help of a nursery nurse student, Leeanne created the gown from lengths of cloth fastened with safety pins and decorated with stapled-on braiding. Once the gown was completed she returned to her imaginative play and continued the story. At the end of the session she chose to record her experience by drawing a picture of the ball, which she shared with her mother at home time. Leeanne's learning covered a number of creative and imaginative experiences. She engaged in imaginative play, used textiles and drew. She demonstrated a variety of attitudes, knowledge and skills. For example, cooperation, perseverance, knowledge of fabrics and their properties, knowledge of fairy tales, fine and gross motor skill. For Leeanne these were not experienced as separate, experienced as a whole.

them. Young children need to preserve, develop and value their own worth and the worth of those around them. This does not mean treating all children in the same way but of ensuring that all children feel valued. If all children are to achieve this the adults who are part of their lives must be aware of:

- the prejudice that exists in society,
- the ways in which beliefs based on prejudice affect children's opportunities to learn and develop their creativity and imagination
- the steps that can be taken to challenge and overcome prejudice and ensure equal opportunities for all children.

The range of abilities evident in any group of children make it extremely unwise to simply assume competence, or lack of it, on the basis of membership of a certain group. The abilities they display may be the result of innate ability but can also be the outcome of encouragement from the adults around them. We need, therefore, to ensure that all children have access to a broad range of experiences.

Valuing children's race, religion, culture, class and ethnicity

The materials, equipment and experiences we offer should reflect a wide variety of cultural experiences. This is especially important for mono-cultural settings where children may not have the opportunity to encounter cultural diversity in their community, and when home cultures emphasize clearly defined roles for each gender. Creative experiences and imaginative play offer children the opportunity to explore lifestyles outside their immediate family and to gain an insight into the lives of others. It is important to avoid reinforcing stereotypes, for example, that all Indian women wear saris, or adopting a 'tourist' approach, such as only showing images of people from ethnic minorities in artificial and exotic settings. The aim is to increase children's understanding by showing images that reflect the real-life experience of families from a variety of cultures.

Stereotypical ideas of class may limit children's access. For example, some forms of creative expression, such as ballet and opera, are seen as not being relevant to working-class children. Children from different religious groups can also find their access curtailed, for instance it is sometimes assumed that children from Muslim families are not allowed to depict the human form. In fact, the depiction of the human form is only prohibited in mosques. There are many wonderful examples of Muslim artists representing the human form, for example in miniatures.

The experiences children have in their homes and communities will affect their uptake of the creative and imaginative experiences we offer. The experience of imaginative and creative play alongside an older sibling or friend can enhance younger children's play. In communities where they are part of an extended family or a network of close friends, young children will often have skills that children of a similar age, without access to these networks, lack.

Valuing children's gender

Young children are interested in gender differences and explore the roles adopted by each. While it is essential that children develop a positive self-image, part of which involves their identification with others of the same gender, we need to make sure that this does not limit their access to creative and imaginative experiences. The challenge is to confront stereotypes which limit access, and offer experiences which extend children's horizons. We need to think carefully about the labels we use, for instance, calling the imaginative play area of a classroom the 'Wendy house' or 'home corner' will not encourage boys to use it. Similarly, we need to monitor children's use of the physical environment to ensure equal access. For example, girls may be reluctant about using construction materials if these have been monopolized by boys and are therefore seen as 'boys' toys'. Bloom and Sosniak (1981) examined longitudinal studies of creative people and found that early experiences which de-emphasized traditional roles were significant.

Valuing children with special educational needs

Children with special needs are sometimes offered a limited curriculum with the view that they need to give all their attention to the acquisition of so-called basic skills – though as we saw in Chapter 1 what could be more basic than the desire to create? However, in many ways the experiences that form the creative and imaginative range have a particular relevance to children with special needs. These experiences encourage an open-ended approach to learning and enable children to use all their senses, including those which may be impaired. When children have a condition such as autism, art and music may offer a means of self-expression and creativity when spoken language fails them. Creative and imaginative experiences can offer children with special educational needs the opportunity to order their understandings and inner worlds and share these with others. Music and dance can express meanings which surmount the need for words.

Example

Anderson, aged 4 years 6 months, was visually impaired. His key worker observed his reluctance to engage in forms of representation which involved fine detail and confined locations, such as drawing while seated at a table. She responded by rearranging the outside space to include large sheets of paper attached to the wall for painting and drawing. Anderson responded with enthusiasm. He concentrated for long periods and returned to his drawings to refine and develop the images (see Figure 3.1). The opportunity to work on a large scale enabled him to make full use of his available sight and the more spacious surroundings allowed him to move without fear of bumping into a person or object. By assessing Anderson's particular needs and altering the way in which he had access to drawing experiences his key worker helped him to engage in an aspect of creative expression he had previously been denied.

Figure 3.1 Anderson engaged in representing a snail.

Children who have marked abilities may also experience difficulties. Marked ability in one part of the creative and imaginative range of experience, for example music, may lead to an over-concentration on that area and neglect of other aspects of creativity.

It is essential to ensure that children with special educational needs are not intentionally or unintentionally excluded. The challenge is to adapt or expand the experience so that everyone who wishes can be involved.

Two- and three-dimensional experiences and the possibilities for learning they offer (see Table 3.1)

Two- and three-dimensional experiences are often referred to as the visual arts. Two-dimensional experiences include:

- drawing – defining shapes and events with line
- painting – defining areas of surface colour
- printing – making marks by pressing
- textiles – creating woven surfaces and fabrics
- photography – creating images with the chemical action of light on film.

Three-dimensional representations include:

- constructions – forming representations by fitting together
- sculpting – forming representations by chiselling or carving
- modelling – working plastic materials into shape.

Experiences under this heading offer opportunities to represent using the elements of art:

- pattern – repetition of shape, colour, light
- texture – characteristics or quality of surface
- colour – hue (property of colour e. g. red, orange), intensity, saturation, brilliance, primary colours (red, yellow, blue) secondary colours (combinations of primary colours – orange, green, and violet)
- line – a mark, stroke, strip, dash
- tone – lightness or darkness, shade
- shape – outline
- form – three-dimensional experience of shape
- space – area between shapes.

Table 3.1 Two- and three-dimensional representations and the opportunities they offer for learning

Experience	Knowledge, understanding, concepts	Skills and abilities
Drawing using a wide range of: • graphic and mark-making tools – fingers, pencils, charcoal, computer • surfaces – different textures and sizes of paper and card, chalk boards, computer screens, permissable walls and pavements • subject matter – physical attributes, abstract concepts such as the sound of a drum, recording movement • investigating marks and the qualities of lines, rubbings	• pattern, shape, line, tone, form, space, proportion • types of drawing materials and equipment • uses materials and equipment • drawing from a range of traditions • how to represent texture, shade, pattern movement, with marks	• observation • interpretation • estimation • measurement • experimentation • investigation • prediction • problem-solving • recollection
Painting using a wide range of: • hues – primary, secondary; shades – pastels, dark, light • sorts of paint – powder, block, natural dyes, ready mixed and self-mixed • techniques for applying paint – fingers, feet, a selection of brushes, marbling, spraying, splashing, stencilling • surfaces – paper and card of different sizes and textures	• colours, tints, shades, density • how to mix a range of colours • how to lighten and darken colours • the properties of paint texture • how to represent forms, texture, movement, colour by using paints	• recording • fine manipulation • gross motor skills • correct use of tools, equipment and materials
Printing using a wide range of: • objects – hands, natural and found materials, raised and embossed • surfaces – paper, card, fabric, walls, clay • forms – patterns (repeated and single), natural shapes, manufactured	• two-dimensional surfaces • the importance of flat surfaces when printing • properties of different surfaces • pattern	• communication • hand and eye coordination • tidiness • carefulness • accuracy • safety

Table 3.1 Continued

Experience	Knowledge, understanding, concepts	Skills and abilities
Textiles using a wide range of: • techniques – plaiting, twisting, winding, sewing, dyeing appliqué, printing, knitting • cloths and threads – wool, canvas, hessian, linen, string cotton, printed materials, raffia, straw, grasses, twigs	• textiles and their properties • weaving and sewing techniques • textiles from a range of cultures and times • use of clothing to represent membership of cultural, social or religious groups	
Photography using a range of: • cameras • light sources and images • light-sensitive paper	• know that cameras can take photographs • light sources • light sensitive paper • how to exclude light • the effect of excluding or increasing light	
Constructing – forming representations by fitting together using a wide range of: • commercial and found materials – bricks, blocks, Lego, wood • different ways of joining – using glue gun, gluing, tying, knotting, hammering, threading, looping, nailing, screwing, brass fastening, paper, clipping, stapling, treasury-tagging, binding, interlocking pieces • different ways of parting – cutting, tearing, sawing, punching hole • different forms – mobiles, collages, models	• names of shapes of the blocks and their relative sizes • properties of paper, wood, card • correct use of tools and implements, glue guns, staplers, scissors, etc. • balance • tessellation and pattern	• joining • parting • measuring • comparing size, shape, height • estimating volume • balancing blocks

Table 3.1 Continued

Experience	Knowledge, understanding, concepts	Skills and abilities
Sculpting – forming representations by chiselling or carving using a wide range of: • materials – wood, salt, sand, stone • tools – hands, fingers, cutlery, saws, commercial tools • techniques – carving, hammering	• properties of materials • effect of removing portions from mass	• coordination of eyes, hands and fingers
Modelling – working plastic materials into shape using a wide range of: • materials – papier mâché, clay, dough • tools – hands, fingers, cutlery, commercial tools • techniques – moulding, pinching, scooping, flattening, rolling thumbing, squeezing, attaching, wedging	• of which materials can be modelled • of the effect of manipulating plastic substances	

Musical experiences and the possibilities for learning they offer (see Table 3.2)

Music is one of the performing arts and includes using voice, sounds, tuned instruments, untuned instruments, etc. to:

- produce musical sounds
- perform
- composing.

Musical experiences offer children the opportunities to explore and represent using the following elements:

- timbre – characteristics or qualities of sound
- texture – the way sounds are put together
- pitch – high/low, higher/lower
- dynamics – volume, loud/quiet, louder/quieter
- tempo – speed, fast/slow, faster/slower, rhythm, pulse
- duration – long/short
- harmony – two or more musical sounds produced together.

to provide:

- structure – the organization of sounds, melody, combining musical phrases, and patterns
- composition – creation and formulation of work.

Dance experiences and the possibilities for learning they offer (see Table 3.3)

This is another performing art and includes using expressive movement to:

- produce dance
- perform dance
- compose dance.

Experiences under this heading offer opportunities to explore and represent using the elements of movement:

- basic actions – travelling, jumping, turning, rolling, balancing
- gesture – using face, fingers, hands, arms, feet
- stillness – frozen movement
- pattern – linking and repeating actions and gestures.

Table 3.2 Musical experiences and the possibilities they offer for learning

Experience	Knowledge, understanding, concepts	Skills and abilities
Producing a wide range of musical sounds and performing by: • using voice and mouth – shouting, humming, singing • body – hand clapping, finger clicking, feet stamping, rubbing • found materials – kitchen utensils, blocks, building textures (gravel, bricks, wood) • homemade instruments • keyboards – piano, organ • percussion – tuned (glockenspiel, bells) untuned (drums, shakers) • wind – trumpets, pipes, whistles • strings – violins, guitars, sitars • interpreting the work of others – from memory and simple scores • playing and performing with others	• things that make a sound • vibration produces sound • different sound effects of wood, strings, skin • tempo, rhythm, pitch, dynamic • names of instruments • correct usage of instruments • awareness of audience and venue • simple pieces and accompaniments • repertoire of songs from a range of cultures and traditions • instruments and music from a range of cultures and traditions	• listening, discriminating and memorizing • experimenting with sounds – turn-taking – voice control (breathing, singing, humming) • being part of a group • plucking, hitting, pressing instruments with accuracy • playing as part of a group – turn taking, patience • cutting, fastening, to make instruments
Composing and recording sound in response to a wide range of stimuli through: • opportunities to experiment with sound • memorizing simple patterns to accompany songs • representing sounds and patterns using – child's own symbols and traditional notation • producing sound effects • improvising musical patterns • composing own pieces of music • recording own music • recording sound in different ways – memory, tape recorders, CD players, own marks, notations and scores	• that sound can be represented by symbols • that musical ideas can be communicated to others • ways in which sound can be represented • names of notes, their values and position of notes on stave • pentatonic scale • that major and minor chords can be related to moods	• recording sounds – operating tape recorders, making marks • reading music using child's symbols, colour coded and traditional notation • interpreting sounds and symbols

Table 3.3 Dance experiences and the possibilities they offer for learning

Experience	Knowledge, understanding, concepts	Skills and abilities
Producing and performing using movement expressively and creatively by: • moving the body – what can the body do and which parts of the body move? • moving in space – level, direction, pathways, sizes • moving in time – dynamics, tempo in terms of time, weight space, flow • moving with others – with a partner, in a group, with an object • moving in response to music and sound • develop a repertoire of movements to express what is heard and felt • dances from different cultures and traditions • interpret and execute movements	• names of parts of body • spatial awareness • direction and position of words – left and right, up and down, backwards and forwards, side to side • sequence words – next, first, last • speed words – fast, slow, quicker • how to move body in a particular sequence of movement • movements related to tempo and mood • music can be interpreted in movement	• jumping and bouncing • swinging and swaying • stretching and arching • turning and bending • spinning and twirling • stepping and skipping • crawling and contracting • stopping and starting
Composing and recording in response to a wide range of stimuli by: • representing stories, music and ideas through dance • representing patterns that move • recording steps and movement using children's own symbols • recording steps and movement using traditional symbols	• movement can be represented by symbols • movement – line, form, pattern • way body moves – hands, feet, arms, legs, whole body • steps • use of symbolic movement • ways of recording movement	• tiptoeing and sliding • wriggling and twisting • rolling and balancing • dashing and diving • galloping and kicking • shaking and squatting • initiating • waiting turn • listening • discriminating

Figure 3.2 A group of 3- and 4-year-olds working with professional dancers to produce a dance that represents their ideas on growth.

Imaginative play experiences and the possibilities for learning they offer (see Table 3.4)

Experiences under this heading offer opportunities to explore and represent:

- actions
- roles
- relationships
- situations
- characters from a variety of sources
- narratives and stories.

Table 3.4 Imaginative play experiences and the possibilities they offer for learning

Experience	Knowledge, understanding, concepts	Skills and abilities
Imitative play – copy *actions* of parents and carers using a wide range of: • small world toys, and puppets • props – real and miniature objects • dressing-up clothes	• suitable clothes for particular roles • sequence and characters of stories • appropriate props for different scenes • use of different body language and verbal • relationship and their responsibilities • household tasks – cooking, phoning	• listening and recalling • observing others • tidying up and dressing • writing, recognizing signs • washing-up, mopping • squeezing and sweeping
Imaginative play – using experiences to create own scenario: • socio dramatic play – based on the adult roles children see around them, for example relationships (mothers), functional roles (shopkeepers) • character roles – based on fantasy characters from television, fairy and folk tales • using realistic props and models • using abstract and unstructured props – cardboard boxes • pretend props – finger for toothbrush • imagined props – miming	• community roles and responsibilities • a story has a beginning, middle and end • how to join in at appropriate times • how to negotiate • how to lead or be led • how to improvise • how to develop a narrative	• fine manipulative skills • gross motor skills • drying up, cleaning • estimating, measuring • caring for clothes • sorting and matching • using face paint • joining in, negotiating • leading and being led

Figure 3.3   Candice, aged 1 year 10 months, and Harry, 1 year 9 months, using their knowledge of adult roles and actions in their play with telephones.

Example

Sabrina, aged 3 years and 2 months, Elizabeth, aged 3 years, Maurice, aged 4 years and 1 month and Teddy, aged 4 years 6 months, were painting alongside each other mixing the colours they wanted using block paints in the primary colours and a selection of brushes. Each was involved in creating their own representation but was also aware of, and interested in, the work of the others. Sabrina was engaged in representing a house, she turned to Maurice:

Sabrina: That doesn't look like a house

Maurice: That's because it's not a house it's a brown bear. I'm trying to get brown but it's gone purple.

Teddy [to Sabrina]: Well that doesn't look like a house it looks like a mermaid, look there's the tail.

Elizabeth: You're looking at it upside down that's the roof! Mermaids have legs !

Teddy: No they don't . . . well, I suppose they might have legs inside their tails

Sabrina: I'll put the windows in . . . now it looks like a house

Maurice: It's the mermaid's house, that's what it is!

Appraising and appreciating and the possibilities for learning they offer (see Table 3.5)

Experiences under this heading offer children opportunities to:

- watch, listen and feel
- respond to and comment on
- to appraise and evaluate
- appreciate.

their own expressions of creativity and imagination and those of others.

Depth

Not only do we need to make sure that children have access to broad and balanced provision, we also need to be aware of the importance of ensuring that children are able to deepen their understanding. There is a danger that in trying to ensure that children have access to the breadth of provision listed above, our approach becomes superficial and they end up with a series of activities rather than the opportunity to delve into an experience. Children need time to explore and opportunities to repeat and return to experiences, so as to deepen their understanding.

Each form of creative and imaginative medium have their own properties and offers their own solutions. Access to differing experiences allows children to increase their understanding by solving problems in different ways. Representing the same experience or idea through the different media enables children to explore it in depth. Using an unlikely medium to represent an image or idea, for instance, drawing a loud sound or making the sound of sunshine, challenges children's thinking and skills. The medium they finally choose reflects:

- their mastery of that medium
- the properties the medium brings to solving the problem they wish to solve.

For example, children can explore and deepen their understanding of pattern by encountering the same concept in a variety of media:

- *pattern you can hear* – music, for instance rhythm – ta, taa ta, taa, ta or repeated phrases in a song
- *pattern that moves* – dance, for instance – up and down, up and down or a sequence of steps
- *pattern you can feel* – texture and textile, for instance – under and over, under and over, in and out, in and out, or the feel of the weave

Table 3.5 Appreciation and appraisal and the possibilities they offer for learning

Experiences	Knowledge, understanding, concepts	Skills and abilities
Opportunities to experience a wide variety of creative and imaginative representations including: • their own • other children • their own culture and tradition • other cultures and traditions • their own time • other times • through recordings and copies • live performance – music, dance • hearing the work of others • paintings, sculpture, drawings	• the properties of material • the elements of art, music, dance • the creative process – for example, in printing • how things are constructed and deconstructed • the values concerns and preoccupations of others • intentions of others and gauging their success • purposes of creative and aesthetic expression • the way representations and artifacts enhance the environment in which we live • the role of dance, music, art in life • the role and work of artists and crafts people • history and cultures • vocabulary to describe and discuss what they see, hear and feel	• listening • watching • feeling • responding • articulating • commenting • critical skills • appraising • evaluating • appreciating • valuing

- *pattern you can see* – draw, model and paint, for instance, light and shade, decoration, repeated sequences of colour or shape.

Children can also deepen their understanding through opportunities to represent their experiences and ideas using action, images, and traditional symbols. Bruner (1982) describes these three ways of processing information as:

1 *The enactive mode* – based on action, learning through doing, for example, children representing fast and slow using their body movements.
2 *The iconic mode* – replacing the action with a drawing or using an image to stand for an object or concept, for example, children representing fast and slow using marks and signs they have devised themselves.
3 *The symbolic mode* – using traditional symbols (musical notation, writing, numbers) for example, children using music notation to represent fast and slow.

Through these modes children are able to produce their own representations, store and retrieve information (see Figure 3.4). At different ages different modes will predominate. For example, young children will readily use actions to represent their experiences, whereas they are less likely to use codes such as music notation. There is sometimes a tendency to neglect the enactive mode as children grow older, but it is important to ensure that all the different modes continue to be available to children as each can offer new insights and deepen understanding.

If children are going to have the opportunity to delve into experiences and deepen their understanding they need:

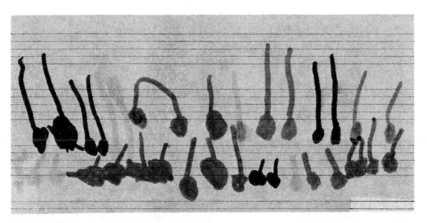

Figure 3.4 Alison, aged 4 years 6 months, who is starting to use traditional musical notation to represent tunes.

- access to materials and equipment
- time to explore materials, equipment
- an understanding of the properties of materials and equipment
- the chance to develop their skills and understanding
- time and opportunities to use their skills and knowledge to create their own representations
- a variety of social contexts: working alone, alongside others, in pairs, in groups.

Differentiation

While it is essential to ensure that all children have the opportunity to experience a wide range of experiences, it is also crucial to recognize that the needs of individual children will vary over time and that the needs of the children in any group will vary at any one time.

Children's learning needs will vary according to their:

- ability
- stage of development
- interest (see Figure 3.5).

In response we need to differentiate the experiences we present, to match the experience we are offering to the learning needs of the individual children we are offering it to. For example, through the questions we ask, and the responses we expect from different children, we can increase the complexity of the experience on offer. By breaking the experience and explanations we give into smaller more manageable steps we can maximize understanding for less able children. Creative and imaginative experiences offer children the freedom to use the materials in an open-ended way. As there is no pre-prescribed end product, individual children are able to use the materials in a way that matches their own learning needs.

The adults expertise is in enabling children to develop mastery and the freedom to explore at their own level by finding ways to develop the skills and concepts children need at the time they need them. To do this we must be sensitive to be aware of:

- what to introduce, and when, by being aware of the typical stages children go through and what is developmentally appropriate (see Chapter 4)
- the processes involved in creativity (see Chapter 5)
- when to intervene and when to stand back (see Chapter 6).

Figure 3.5 We need to match what we offer to the interests of individual children. Georgia, aged 3 years 10 months. The caption under the representation reads 'Georgia was fascinated by the stuffed owl [she asked] "was it real?" She represented it using pen, buttons and feathers. She remembered to draw its "beak, wings, and talons"'.

Conclusion

Children are not empty vessels. They have their own ideas and thoughts, their own desire to create. Our responsibility is to ensure that we build on children's current skills and understandings and expand this by providing new opportunities that develop their attitudes, skills and knowledge across a broad range of experiences. But if our work with children is not to be limited to covering a list of activities we need a clear understanding of how children's creativity and imagination develops. The next two chapters will address this.

Summary

This chapter has:

- addressed the dangers of a narrow approach that leads to depressed thinking
- established the importance of access to a wide range of experiences
- stressed the importance of access for all children
- defined the range of experiences we wish children to explore
- discussed the importance of breadth and balance, depth and differentiation.

Further reading

Bruner, J. (1982) 'What is representation?', in M. Roberts and J. Tamburrini (eds) *Child Development 0–5*. Edinburgh: Holmes McDougall.
Bruner explains the concept of the enactive, iconic and symbolic modes.
Garvey, C. (1977) *Play*. London: Fontana.
Garvey looks at the ways in which play helps children to learn.
Morgan, M. (1988) *Art 4–11*. Oxford: Blackwell.
This book offers ideas and suggestions for developing children's art experiences.
Siraj-Blatchford, I. (1994) *The Early Years: Laying the Foundations for Racial Equality*. Stoke-on-Trent: Trentham Books.
Siraj-Blatchford argues that racism is inherent in society and damaging to all.

Things to think about

- Were you aware of the wide range of experiences covered by two- and three-dimensional representation, music, dance and imaginative play?
- Do the children for whom you are responsible have access to a wide range of activities?
- Look at the range of experiences listed. Can you add more?
- Do you think some are more important than others? If so which and why?

Part Two

How *do creativity and imagination develop?*

We sing before we talk.

Trevarthen 'Music in Mind', Channel Four,
transcript (1996)

4

The development of creativity and imagination from birth to 6 years

Introduction

This chapter will explore:

- the interconnectedness of all aspects of development
- Bruner's concept of the spiral curriculum
- the development of imaginative play
- the development of two-dimensional representation, in particular drawing, painting and textiles
- the development of three-dimensional representation
- the development in music
- the development in dance
- the importance of developmentally appropriate approaches.

The interconnectedness of all aspects of development

In the last chapter we looked at the importance of ensuring that children have access to a wide range of experience through which to develop their creativity and imagination. Imagination is linked to development, the ability to imagine increases as children get older (see Table 4.1). Creativity can

(a)

(b)

Figure 4.1 Children's abilities vary, as can be seen in these drawings by (a) a boy aged 4 years 3 month and (b) a girl aged 4 years 3 months.

occur at any age. As we established in Chapter 2, it is about connecting the previously unconnected. As we learn and develop our ability to make connections increases – we have more information to combine and more skills to employ. Creativity is a way of thinking, a process, and we will look at this process in detail in the next chapter.

Imagination and creativity are both influenced by learning and experience and, as we can see in Figure 4.1, children of the same age may show a marked variation in their abilities. Children's development is dependent on a number of components:

- *maturation* – children's genetically pre-programmed inheritance
- *learning* – the experiences and opportunities children have to practise
- *social* – the culture, race, social class, of individual families or communities and their expectations for children.

All aspects of development are interlinked, children develop as a whole, not in separate pieces. Each aspect of development interacts and overlaps to facilitate the development of imagination and creativity. For example:

1 *Cognitive development* The development of the imagination and creativity are part of children's cognitive development. Many of our theories about cognitive development come from Piaget (1926/51). His work has been criticized for providing a model of development which underestimates young children's thinking powers and the role of the adult as educator (Trevarthen 1995). But the emphasis he puts on children creating their own understanding of the world through their experience is useful. Piaget introduced the idea of stages of development and of sequential changes in children's mental structures. As children progress through these stages their ability to engage in creative and imaginative experiences increases. In turn, the projection into an imaginary world stretches their conceptual abilities and involves a development in their abstract thought. The complexity involved in this process makes imagination the highest level of early development (Vygotsky 1978).

2 *Perceptual development* The development of creativity and imagination are also part of children's perceptual development. We perceive the world through our senses. As their senses of sight, hearing, and touch develop, children's ability to perceive and understand the world increases. They develop tactile, visual, auditory, spatial and movement perception and this development has an impact on many of the experiences we identified in Chapter 3. For instance, babies cannot synchronize their eyes, but by about the sixth month they are able to reach for an object they can see and at about a year can follow rapidly moving

objects. By the age of 3-years-old children's visual perception is similar to that of an adult. This ability to see with understanding has a direct impact on their ability to represent.

3 *Physical development* Young children use their physical abilities to explore the world and reach interesting objects. Babies start their explorations with everyday things and mastery of materials. How can objects and materials be used? Can they be thrown, draped, crunched up? What are they used for? As their ability to sit, crawl and walk increases children see the world from new angles and their view of the world widens. Once children become confident walkers their hands are free to explore more of the world around them. As they are no longer concentrating on remaining upright, children are able to give their full attention to exploring objects and material. Objects previously unreachable can be taken down and explored. Increased manipulative skill means that objects can be twisted and turned, materials can be tipped and poured. Physical development, especially the growth in the children's fine manipulative skills has a profound influence on their ability to represent. From birth children develop their ability to hold and grasp. This growing physical competence is reflected in the range of lines, shapes and form that appear in their creative and imaginative representations.

4 *Language development* Language, imagination and creativity all involve the ability to represent experience symbolically, whether this is a spoken word standing for an object or an empty yoghurt pot standing for a cup of tea. The listening skills and attention to details that are part of most forms of creative and imaginative representation are also crucial to language and literacy development. As children's use of spoken language develops they are better able to express their thoughts and ideas to others. This enhances their imaginative play and enables the development of complex story lines which involve negotiation with others. In turn, the narratives they develop through imaginative play inform the stories they tell and write. Writing involves the fine manipulative skills that develop through exposure to many forms of creative expression. Trevarthen (1995) has drawn our attention to the link between music and language. Babies recognize and respond to the musical elements of speech, rhythm, accents, dynamics and timbre, and from this develops their ability to use and understand spoken language. Songs which engage young children usually have a clear beginning, middle and end and as this structure becomes well known to children it provides them with a 'rhythm story' to follow and anticipate. Familiarity with this structure helps them to understand the structure of written stories that they will encounter later.

5 *Social and emotional development* As children's social and emotional

awareness and skills develop, they are able to join with others to express their creativity and imagination, for example, they develop the self-discipline and cooperative skills involved in working as part of a group. In return creative and imaginative experiences offer children the opportunity to express themselves and reflect which enhances their social and emotional development. The opportunity to explore a wide variety of roles in imaginative play, and to experience the art, music and dance of different cultures, develops children's understandings of their own and other cultures.

Example

At a week old Marie was already starting her journey into creativity and imagination:

- She widened her eyes as her father sang to her, engaged by the sound
- She tried to imitate her aunt as she stuck out her tongue
- She was soothed by the rocking and swaying movements her grandmother used
- She gazed intently at the pattern of the lining in her crib and appeared to be attracted by the light coming through the window
- Marie nuzzled into her mother's neck as she held her and seemed to be taking delight in the feel of her mother's skin.

The spiral curriculum

Children's development should not be seen as progression up a ladder. Bruner's (1977) concept of a spiral is a more useful image. As their abilities evolve young children are able to explore an ever-widening world. They do not leave behind the interests and understandings of earlier stages but add on to these to develop an increasingly complex view of the world and their relationship to it. For Bruner, there are basic themes at the core of all subjects. Deeper understanding comes from learning to use these in progressively more complex forms. For example, the young child using her fingers to spread spilt food is developing an understanding of the way in which marks are made and she will build on this to develop an understanding of drawing and other forms of representation. Learning experiences that are offered to children must reflect their current level of development and offer the possibility of further development. They must be developmentally appropriate.

The development of imaginative play (see Table 4.1)

It used to be thought that children's imaginative play developed through similar stages to that of other forms of play:

1 onlooker – watching as others engaged in play
2 solitary – playing by themselves
3 parallel – playing alongside another child
4 cooperative – playing with another child.

However the work of people such as Goldschmied and Jackson (1994) has shown that very young children demonstrate that they can engage in cooperative play. For example, given opportunities children under a year will offer objects to other babies and look for the same object that they have seen another child exploring. It is perhaps better to think of these as styles of play. Each is present at each stage of development, and at some stages more of a particular style will predominate.

From their first year children imitate the people around them and from this tendency imitative and imaginative play develops. Imitative play involves children copying or imitating. Initially this will occur during an experience, for example, babies will copy the facial expression of carers. Later this will involve reconstructing the event after it has taken place, for example children using the gestures and movements involved in their sleep routine while playing with a doll. As they grow, their ability to imagine influences the nature of their play. Hiding games where the adult hides her face behind her hands and then removes them to reappear, encourage children to imagine what does not exist. Imaginative play involves making up and internalizing actions; children are not simply copying what they have seen but adding their own ideas. Play based on relational roles becomes increasingly complex as children develop and the narratives which are created include more characters and episodes.

The role of fantasy increases as children develop and the scenarios they create are no longer restricted to their first-hand experience of the world but include characters and events from stories and television. Sometimes children's fantasy play is discouraged. It is seen as an avoidance of the real world and as reinforcing stereotypical images. For example, super-hero play such as Power Rangers is thought to encourage violence, and fairy tales to reinforce beliefs about physical beauty. However, Paley (1988) presents a very persuasive argument for allowing super heroes and Bettelheim's (1976) work highlighted the importance of traditional fairy tales in children's development and the role of particular tales at particular stages in children's development. The contribution they make to children's creativity and imagination means that a suitable place must be found for

Table 4.1 The development of imaginative play

	Children:
Birth–1 year	• imitate, or copy, the actions and behaviour of adult during an event, for example, copies adult's expression • respond to adult-initiated imitating • enjoy playing games involving hiding the face
1–2 years	• imitate the actions or behaviour of adults after an event • are interested in discovering the use of everyday objects • begin to develop the ability to symbolize and are able to use realistic and miniature items to support symbolic play, for example, tea sets • may use a transitional object. For example, a teddy, to represent their mother in her absence
2–3 years	• may use a transitional object to represent themselves • enjoy copying the actions and behaviour of children of the same age • use scenarios from everyday life in their play, for example, making dinner • will use a transitional object which shares some characteristic with the object being represented • are interested in role play and will act out the roles they see around them. • use actions to indicate the role they are adopting, for example, holding the baby doll to indicate that they are the mother
3–4 years	• start to introduce a story line, or narrative into their play • will play alongside other children engaged in the same play theme, for example, firefighters • will play cooperatively as part of a group to act out a narrative
4–5 years	• are interested in character roles, for example, from fantasy such as fairy tales, or television • are able to use as a transitional object, something which shares no characteristic with the imagined object, for example, a block can represent money • revisit imaginative play themes with increased complexity
At 6 years	• are able to engage in pretence; they need no props to support their imaginative play, for example, they can mime brushing teeth • act out increasingly complex narratives in their imaginative play; there are more characters, action, and items in each story line

creativity and imagination means that a suitable place must be found for these aspects of imaginative play.

Vygotsky's (1978) observation of young children and the theories he developed from these, indicate the crucial role of imagination in the development of the human mind. The ability to imagine is what makes us uniquely human. Until the second year he found little evidence of this ability. The emergence of the imagination appeared to be connected with the frustrations children experienced when their desires were not immediately gratified. For the baby, desires are straightforward and either quickly gratified or forgotten, but as children grow this changes. Their wishes and aspirations become more complex, less realizable and less capable of instant fulfilment. For example, they may want to pour the tea out as they have seen adults do and become angry and frustrated when, for safety reasons, they are not allowed to. Imaginative play develops when children experience this frustrating gap between their needs and the gratification of these needs. But while this desire cannot be realized in the real world it can be satisfied in the imaginative world, they can pretend to pour the tea and offer it to their parents. The imaginative world children create enables them to realize in their imagination the things that cannot be realized in reality. Through imaginative play children resolve the tensions of every-day life.

Objects may support the imaginative process as 'transitional objects'. These objects no longer have the meaning they have in the real world but are used to represent a missing object. For example, children may use stones to represent money while playing shops. The stones act as a prop or pivot (Vygotsky 1978). Without the stones to help them the children would find it hard to engage in the imaginative process. Initially transitional objects need to share many characteristics with the object being imagined. But gradually the need for physical similarity between the actual object

---

Example

Bubbie was a toy rabbit which Emily has had since she was a week old. Emily slept happily with Bubbie present, without Bubbie, Emily found the separation from her parents hard. When she stayed with her grandparents Bubbie came too. The smell and feel of Bubbie comforted Emily and represented her parents and home, allowing her to hold on to them in her imagination. By the age of 2 Emily was using Bubbie to represent herself. When given a biscuit Emily pretended to feed it to Bubbie before eating it herself and when Emily was reprimanded Bubbie was told off in turn by Emily! Bubbie also acted as a companion, for example, Emily talked to Bubbie as she lay in her cot.

and the imagined object decreases. Eventually, children no longer require an actual object to support their imaginative play but can pretend the object is there.

Bruce (1987) draws on Winnicott's (1971) different use of the term 'transitional object'. For Winnicott a transitional object appears to be used by children to represent their mother when she is absent, and this can help children to separate from her. Bruce has developed this idea to include children's use of a transitional object to stand for the child herself, or as a companion for the child.

The development of two-dimensional representation

From birth children are exposed to visual imagery. They are surrounded by the images of others. Children's ability to represent in two dimensions has sometimes been seen as simply the move from non-representational images (drawings or paintings that do not look like the items being represented, at least in the view of adults!) to representational images (drawings and images which resemble the items being represented). Piaget (1951) identified stages in this process:

1 *Fortuitous realism*: Children notice similarities between the random marks they have made and objects they have seen.
2 *Intellectual realism*: Children represent what they know, not what they see.
3 *Visual realism*: Children represent what they see, not what they know.

Matthews sees the development of two-dimensional representation as a much more complex process and argues that visual realism is apparent at an early stage (Matthews 1994). Children's early representations are more purposeful than Piaget's theory suggests. For example, they show an awareness of composition by targeting new marks in a way that relates to existing marks. When they do this children are showing awareness of the arrangement of lines and the spaces between them as seen in Figure 4.3, see pages 62–5. Tahlia paused and looked at the drawing before she made each line and appeared to be placing each line with reference to the existing lines. For example, the marks at the bottom of the page all intersect at a central point.

The images children produce are not only to do with representing static and photographically accurate images but also about exploring and representing movement and the qualities of materials (Matthews 1994). So, for example, a child may draw lots of streaky lines next to his car and say 'this car is going very, very fast' as Tarek has done in Figure 4.2.

Figure 4.2 Tarek, aged 3 years, 'a car going very, very fast'.

Early representations are closely connected with children's growing awareness of their physical actions and movement. Children 's images can focus on representing various aspects and view-points. They may highlight:

- *configurative aspects* – to do with space
- *dynamic aspects* – to do with action (as in Figure 4.2)
- *specific view points* – drawn from a particular view point
- *object specific* – to do with the main features of an object.

A single representation may include one or a combination of the list above, the deciding factor being which features of the object, experience, feeling or idea are important to the child concerned.

The development of drawing (see Table 4.2)

Drawing guides children's observations of the world (Matthews 1994). From birth babies are interested in pattern and are attracted to those which show marked contrasts of light and dark and are related to the features of the human face. Early representations are a way of leaving one's mark. Children build on the early marks they have made with food and drink with their fingers and hands when they are given access to graphic

Table 4.2   The development of drawing

	Children:
Birth–1 year	• imitate actions and movements using their whole body • are aware of patterns which have strong contrasts and resemble the human face • make intentional marks, for example, with food using finger and hand • are aware that movements result in a mark
1–2 years	• make a variety of marks, sometimes described as scribbling • are aware that different movements make different marks • grip pen or crayon using palm of hand • make marks which record and represent the movement of their bodies and other objects • draw overlapping and layered marks
2–3 years	• uses pincer grip to hold graphic materials • produce continuous line and closed shape to represent inside and outside • combine lines and shapes • produce separate but linked shapes
3–4 years	• name marks, and symbolic representation is emerging • experiment with the variety of marks that can be made by different graphic materials, tools and surfaces • unaided, use a circle plus lines to represent person, often referred to as a 'tadpole person' • start to produce visual narratives
4–5 years	• are able to produce a range of shapes and sometimes combines them, for example, to produce a sun • draw shapes and figures that appear to float in space on the page • draw figures which include more details, such as arms, legs, hands, fingers, eyebrows • subdivide space on page to show higher and lower
At 6 years	• draw figures that are grounded and uses lines for ground and sky • display depth by making figures in the distance smaller to indicate further away • include more detail in their drawings, for example, windows, door and chimneys on buildings • drawings have more narrative features, for example, may feature a number of episodes from the same story

materials. Matthews links these early stages, sometimes referred to as scribbles, to the babbling stage of language development. Early drawing, like early language is about exploring rules. Marks made in early drawing are closely connected to movement. The marks children are making at this stage reflect three basic arm movements:

1 *vertical arch* – made by a swiping gesture with a downward circular action
2 *horizontal arch* – made by a wiping or fanning gesture
3 *push and pull* – made by a reaching and grasping gesture.

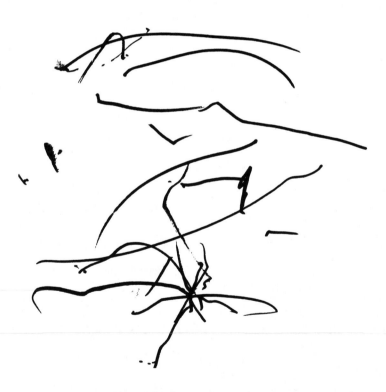

Figure 4.3 a–e Examples of the development of drawing
(a) Lines over-lapping and intersecting at a central point – girl, aged 1 year 10 months

From these marks and movements children develop a continuous line which is later used to produce a closed shape. By separating a space from the surrounding area they can represent inside and outside. The closed shape will take on a variety of meanings, depending on children's wishes. For example, in Figure 4.3(b) the closed mark represents 'my tummy button'.

The shapes and patterns that children develop in their drawings are initially personal to them and later they develop images that can be shared with others and used to communicate thoughts, feelings and ideas. Kellogg's (1970) work has shown that children from a wide variety of cultures create similar symbols in the early stages of representation. As they develop children's drawings show increasing detail and control (see Figure 4.3 a–e). This is reflected in their ability to translate the shapes they see into marks on the page.

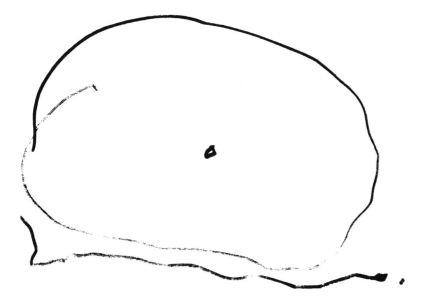

(b) Closed shapes – boy, aged 2 years 3 months

(c) Circles plus lines used to represent a person – boy, aged 3 years 5 months

(d) People with arms, legs, and hands under a sun – girl, aged 4 years 6 months

(e) 'My mummy dancing with her hair flying out' – girl, aged 5 years.

The development of painting (see Table 4.3)

Painting allows us to explore light and colour. Colour affects us all and this is reflected in the language we use. We talk about being green with envy, feeling blue or seeing red. The use of colour allows children to dramatically increase the information they can give through their representations. At birth babies are able to distinguish bright and dark and have some perception of colour especially bright, clear colours such as red.

Early encounters with paint will concentrate on its tactile qualities the potential to squeeze and manipulate thick paint, the trickling effect of thin paint. These explorations are crucial, as during this period children are developing mastery of the paint and an understanding of the techniques that can be used to control it. Once these skills have been acquired children can use paint for their own purposes. Later children explore paint's ability to cover areas of surface, to overlap, to mix and to layer. According to Matthews, children's fascination with layering paint may be to do with early attempts to represent three dimensions (Matthews 1994). As technical skills develop children are able to place blocks of colour alongside each

Table 4.3   The development of painting

	Children:
Birth–1 year	• explore texture using all their senses. For example, the texture of food • are aware of colour and light, especially clear, bright colours such as red
1–2 years	• explore the textural qualities of paint using feet, hands, mouth • use hands, feet and fingers to manipulate paint on surfaces • are aware of colour in their environment • use paint to make intentional marks
2–3 years	• use paint to code separate marks • ask the name of the colour of objects and knows the names of some colours • are able to sort and match colour hues
3–4 years	• know the names of primary colours • are interested in mixing their own colours • enjoy exploring a range of brushes and surface • use paint to produce separate and overlapping blocks of colour • are able to sort and match colour shades
4–5 years	• are able to name secondary colours • are able to mix their own colours, know that adding white lightens a colour and that black darkens it • choose the appropriate brushes and paper for task, for example, know that thin brush will produce fine line • use paint to produce representational forms and patterns • describe their intentions, and comments on outcomes in their painting • are starting to match colours used in painting to colours seen, when representing realism
At 6 years	• include fine detail in their paintings • are able to mix a wide range of colours with exactness • place small areas of colour accurately • place colours side by side with precision

other to create a patchwork effect. Paint is also used in a linear fashion to draw. The ability to handle paint and to draw accurately gradually come together, and children are then able to use paint to create images that draw on its unique qualities. An interest in mixing paint is present from an early stage and children need opportunities to practise these skills. As their mixing skills improve children should have the chance to mix their own colours in response to what they see.

Computer paint programmes are a useful addition to their range of experiences. Children quickly learn that the angle of the painting and the painting surface are different. The screen may only show part of the painting movement. They also quickly realize that there is no possibility for paint to mix and run.

Textural awareness and textiles (see Table 4.4)

Textiles are part of our lives, the clothes we wear, the bedding we curl up under and the curtains and rugs we use in our homes. Our awareness of textiles starts with our awareness of texture. Some of our earliest memories may be about the feel of things – the prickly woollen jumper we did not want to wear, the silky edge of the blanket that we rubbed as we went to sleep. Children are surrounded by textiles from their birth and discriminate from a young age between textures they like, which soothes them, and those that are uncomfortable.

The texture, touch and feel of material and fabrics are important to us. At birth the mouth is the most sensitive part of the body and children use this to explore texture and form. Later children will use their hands, as well as their mouth, to explore texture and discover whether a surface is:

- hard or soft
- rough or smooth
- cold or hot
- itchy or silky
- fluffy or jagged.

In previous generations, and in many communities today, the production of fabric and clothes were part of the life of every home. Clothing is part of our culture and Trevarthen's research suggests that as young as 9 months old babies are aware of clothes (Trevarthen 1995). As children grow they become aware of the clothes appropriate to different situations. The clothes we wear become an expression of who we are and are very much part of our identity.

As children's physical skills increase their ability to produce textiles for themselves develops. Textile production introduces the child to the functional aspects of textiles as well as a form of creative expression.

Table 4.4 The development of textural awareness and textile skills

	Children:
Birth–1 year	• are soothed by the feel and touch of carers skin and hair • use their mouth to explore the texture and feel of food and objects. • use hands to explore the fabrics they are wrapped in, their soft toys, the skin and hair of carers • take pleasure in certain textures and experience discomfort from others
1–2 years	• are aware of the different textures of clothing and bedding and show marked preferences • enjoy feeling and comparing different textures and textiles • are aware of the textural qualities of favourite clothes, blankets, toys • are aware of clothes for different situations, for example, a coat when it's cold • enjoy trying to dress by themselves
2–3 years	• enjoy dressing and undressing dolls and pretend to wash clothes • are able to describe surface textures in simple terms, for example, describing a woollen jumper as prickly • are aware of the need to wear certain clothes for a particular occasion, for example, an apron for painting
3–4 years	• are interested in what clothes, toys, etc., are made from • can discuss the qualities of different material, for example, towel as rough, velvet as smooth • are interested in the properties of different materials, for example, waterproof clothing • are able to explore different surface textures through rubbings, and can sort objects by feel • are interested in textile techniques of construction, for example, sewing and plaiting
4–5 years	• can produce textiles using simple weaving, printing, dyeing, etc., techniques • have a wide vocabulary to describe different textures • use lengths of fabric to produce simple garments
At 6 years	• have greater skill in production of textiles. For example, can manipulate waft under and over accurately while weaving • use sewing to produce simple clothes for dolls and toys • are interested in decoration and detail • are aware that clothes are worn to indicate membership of cultural, social and religious communities

Table 4.5 The development of three-dimensional awareness and representation

	Children:
Birth–1 year	• experience the world in three dimensions • handle, feel and manipulate three-dimensional objects and materials using hands, fingers and mouth • use eyes to explore form • enjoy manipulating food • experience three-dimensional construction such as mobiles
1–2 years	• heap objects and demolish structures • mix and stir flour and water • manipulate dough and clay • tear and crunch paper and card
2–3 years	• construct using ready-made forms, for example, blocks, bricks, boxes • use construction materials, such as blocks, horizontally, for example, will line up blocks to create a road • stack, roll and line up objects • use hands to roll, pinch, coil dough and clay
3–4 years	• construct using raw materials such as clay, wood, card • use hands and tools to manipulate materials and create forms • add features to surfaces using fingers and tools • use construction materials vertically, for example, will balance blocks to create towers
4–5 years	• use fingers and tools to create forms that represent ideas • engage in complex block play, for example, use blocks to create a structure that can be entered • are interested in decorating the surface of malleable materials such as clay • can record constructions through drawings
At 6 years	• are aware of a variety of natural and manufactured forms • express their own ideas in a variety of media • can produce plans for three-dimensional structures and follow them

The development of three-dimensional representation (see Table 4.5)

We experience the world through three dimensions, height, width and depth. Babies have an awareness of this from a young age. For example, babies are aware of size consistency, they know that objects remain the same size as they move towards us even though they look as if they are becoming larger (Karmiloff-Smith 1994). This is often forgotten and we limit children's access to representing in three dimensions, giving preference to representing the world they experience in two dimensions. Construction and malleable materials give children opportunities to represent the world in three-dimensional forms.

Gura's research on children's block play (Gura 1992) shows how access to these materials enables children to develop their representations of the world in ways which two-dimensional materials cannot match. Although blocks do not have the fluidity of paint or the fineness of drawing with a pencil, they can be used just as creatively as these or other art materials. Blocks can be moved and rearranged an infinite number of times to produce the most satisfying design, whereas paint, for example, once applied to paper becomes a permanent feature of the work.

Models and constructions can have a top, bottom, sides, front and back, as well as an inside and outside. If they are large enough they can be walked around and entered. By working together children can create sophisticated designs.

Children often use a wide range of objects in their three-dimensional representations, not necessarily materials specifically designed for the purpose. Most adults who live with young children have experience of chairs and tables being turned into space ships and boats, tins from the cupboard being used to create towers. While these representations may not always occur at convenient times they are evidence of a creative and imaginative approach to the use of materials and growing confidence in three-dimensional representation.

The development of music (see Table 4.6)

Music is a form of communication that is spiritual, emotional and intellectual. The steady pulse of the body, the rhythm of steps, the heart beat, means that the rhythm of music is natural to us. And we are born with the most portable of instruments, the human voice. Babies in the womb respond to sound and at birth are able to distinguish their mother's voice. They turn towards familiar voices, experiment and expand the range of sounds they can make. Young children are fascinated by the sound properties of objects – one of the reasons why dropping rattles is so attractive! Long before they can talk babies can match the pitch and chant of songs (Trevarthen 1995).

There is a natural connection between music and body movement. A

Table 4.6 The development of musical awareness and skills

	Children:
Birth–1 year	• are sensitive to dynamics and timbre, for example, are startled by loud sound • respond to the human voice and recognise the sound of the mother's voice • read emotion in voices • are comforted by lullabies and engage in vocal play • associate sounds with things
1–2 years	• imitate adult vocalizations and melody and rhythm appear in them • engage in musical performances • are interested in the source of sounds and manipulate materials to produce sound, for example, tin lids • use both hands when making sounds
2–3 years	• attempt to imitate sound or tune and use melody patterns from learnt songs spontaneously • explore the sound potential of household objects • can use hands independently and clap to rhythm in song
3–4 years	• are developing voice control • can play simple rhythm instruments and respond to a suggested rhythm • can name familiar tunes, know and join in with some songs • are aware of beat, tempo, melody and pitch
4–5 years	• know some basic concept – high/low, long/short, fast/slow • know names of range of musical instruments • can sing complete songs from memory with a degree of accuracy • sing spontaneously and enjoy group singing • listen to recordings with help
At 6 years	• have a sense of pitch, rhythm, melody • can demonstrate some musical concepts • sing with increased accuracy • have a sense of harmony • can use hands and feet independently

baby responds with its whole body to music and this is reinforced by the apparently instinctive rocking that adults engage in as they croon and sing to it. Mothers introduce babies to the popular music of the day. As well as singing lullabies they will sing and dance with their babies to the radio and records. Between 6 and 12 months babies will sing to others if their audience is a familiar, appreciative adult. They are becoming aware of performing music, albeit at a rudimentary level (Trevarthen 1995).

By the age of 2 children's auditory perception for high-frequency tones is comparable to an adult's and later development focuses on making sense of what they hear. As children grow they become more competent in their music making as their ability to use and respond to musical elements increases.

From a young age children, in Western European culture, are aware of recorded music and the desire to record their own music increases as they grow. At first they will use their own symbols to represent sounds but gradually they will be able to understand and use traditional notation.

The development of dance (see Table 4.7)

Dance is the art form of movement. Movement becomes dance when it includes creativity and imagination. While all dance is movement not all movement is dance (Davies 1995). In dance the body is the instrument and to use this instrument to the full, children need opportunities to develop and practise a range of actions and gestures. Movement is the natural response to music and young babies respond to it with a range of movement. They seem unable to remain still!

Babies' gestures, facial expressions and movements are eloquent and can be used to convey a wide range of feelings. They are mimics and copy the people around them. Adults' voices and gestures are endlessly fascinating to babies and opportunities to imitate with a receptive adult are crucial to their development. Babies are introduced to dance at a young age and by 4 months will show signs of dance like play in response to music (Trevarthen 1995).

The 2-year-old who shouts 'Watch me dance!' is already very aware of the role of audience and spectator. Children gradually learn which movements work well together and ways in which these movements can be joined to together to produce a dance. As I write I can see the 4-year-olds in the nursery garden performing the Spice Girls' latest dance routine with an alarming degree of accuracy! This knowledge of movements and the ways in which they are creatively combined to produce dance can lead children into composition.

As they grow children's movements become increasingly controlled, fluid and graceful and this is reflected in the quality of their dance.

Table 4.7 The development of dance

	Children:
Birth–1 year	• are sensitive to dynamics, for example, are startled by loud sounds • respond to music with their whole body by bouncing, rocking and swaying • are aware of and interested in movement for its own sake and explore own movements • imitate gestures and expression • read emotions in facial expressions and have a repertoire of eloquent expressions and gestures
1–2 years	• dance when asked, if music playing • jump up and down • are fascinated with mirrors and watch their own expressions • are becoming more confident in walking and running
2–3 years	• move arms and legs with some synchronization • walk smoothly and at various speeds • will respond the tempo of a piece of the music • join in songs involving finger play and action rhymes
3–4 years	• start to experiment with different body movements in response to music • enjoy exploring and practising movements for its own sake • march in time to music and walk on tip-toes • can switch from one movement to another during dance
4–5 years	• are able to master a wider range of movements, for example, skips, hops and forward jumps • move with increased awareness of rhythm • are able to use movement to interpret music, for example, will respond to 'sad' music • perform simple dance steps
At 6 years	• are able to improvise movements in response to the tempo of the music • are able to remember steps, for example, in folk dance • are able to work with others to compose, practise and perfect a dance • move with greater fluidity and grace • are able to perform increasingly complex series of movements • display increased narrative in their choreography

Conclusion

The most effective way to meet the needs of individual children is through experiences that are developmentally appropriate. As in all aspects of their development children's character and disposition will play a part in how individual children respond to the opportunities offered to them. Some children simply enjoy particular aspects of imaginative play, or two- and three-dimensional representation, or music or dance more than others. But the attitudes and knowledge of the adults around them are crucial. If they are surrounded by informed adults who give clear messages that creative and imaginative experiences are to be valued and enjoyed children's development will be enhanced.

Summary

This chapter has looked at:

- the importance of developmentally appropriate experiences
- the interrelatedness of all aspects of development
- how we are born with the desire to explore the world
- Bruner's concept of a 'spiral curriculum'
- the role of imitation in the development of imaginative play and other aspects of creativity
- the development of drawing, painting, textile awareness, three-dimensional awareness, music and dance.

Further reading

Bruner, J. (1977) *The Process of Education.* Cambridge, Mass.: Harvard University Press.
Bruner explains the concept of the spiral curriculum.
Davies, M. (1995) *Helping Children to Learn Through a Movement Perspective.* London: Hodder and Stoughton.
Davies explores the role played by movement in the lives of children.
Gura, P. (1992) *Exploring Learning: Young Children and Block Play.* London: Paul Chapman.
Gura and others explore block play and its contribution to children's learning.

Matthews, J. (1994) *Helping Children to Draw and Paint in Early Childhood*. London: Hodder and Stoughton.
Matthews draws on original research from three unique longitudinal studies and his work with nursery and infant children to interpret the meaning of children's drawings and paintings.
Vygotsky, L. (1978) *Mind in Society*. Cambridge, Mass.: Harvard University Press.
In Chapter 7, Vygotsky examines the role of play in development.

Things to think about

- Can you remember your early experiences of art and music?

- How did the adults around you respond?

- How do you think that influenced your development?

5

The creative process ·

Introduction

This chapter will:

- establish the importance of understanding the creative process
- investigate the processes involved in mastering equipment and materials
- explore the processes involved in exploring ideas
- explore a model of the creative process in young children
- stress the importance of errors
- examine Athey's work on schema.

The importance of understanding the creative process

In Chapter 1, I described creativity as a way of thinking, a process. The ability to think creatively, to connect the previously unconnected in a meaningful way, is apparent at all ages and stages of development. The creative process involves selection, reasoning and hard thinking. It involves a condensation of perceptual information and its transformation into a new form (McKellar 1957).

Creative people are not passive. While we may value creativity and wish to encourage it, creative children can be viewed as troublesome by some because they question and want to explore possibilities rather than accepting the view of the adults around them.

This may be hard for the adults concerned. We may:

- feel that children are threatening our authority by not accepting our viewpoint
- lack confidence in our knowledge, understanding and skills and therefore unwilling to let children move beyond the prepared lesson plan
- feel that a state of anarchy will ensue! It is important to remember that we are not talking about uninhibited self-expression. The creative process is about intellectual freedom, the freedom to explore ideas, not the freedom to do what you want.
- welcome the children's curiosity but feel pressurized by time constraints to rush the children on to the next learning objective.

Certainly, the curriculum demands at Key Stage 1 can make it appear that the best solution is to pre-package children's learning to ensure that the whole curriculum is covered. However, we do this at our peril. In Chapter 1 we looked at the value of creativity and imagination, and notwithstanding how hard it is, if we believe that they are crucial to children's current development and to future societies, we must ensure that children have the time and space to engage in the creative process.

There need be no conflict between Key Stage 1 requirements and encouraging children to engage in the creative process. For example, in order to fulfil the Art Key Stage 1 Programmes of Study for 'Investigation and Making' and 'Knowledge and Understanding' children require opportunities to:

- respond to ideas, methods or approaches
- record responses to what has been experienced, observed or imagined
- gather resources to stimulate and develop ideas
- explore and use two- and three-dimensional media
- recognize differences and similarities
- experiment with tools and techniques
- review, evaluate and modify.

Again, in the Music Key Stage 1 Programme of Study 'Performing and Composing' and 'Listening and Appraising' children require opportunities to:

- improvise musical patterns
- explore, create, select and organize sounds
- respond and evaluate performances.

And finally, in the Dance requirements for Key Stage 1, children need opportunities to:

- explore moods and feelings
- to develop their responses to music through dance.

The National Curriculum requirements are reflected in the stages of the creative process we will be looking at. In order to meet our responsibilities to children we have to give them opportunities to engage in the creative process.

If we are to encourage the creative process we must understand as much as we can about it. There appear to be two main stages in this process. Children need to:

- explore and master equipment, materials and ideas
- use this mastery to make new connections.

Exploring and developing mastery of materials and equipment

Before children can use materials and equipment for their own purposes and express their own creativity they need to gain mastery over equipment and develop a range of skills. Sometimes children can short-circuit this by gaining the help of someone who has already achieved mastery. But if they are not to be always dependent on others children need to develop their own mastery.

Hutt (1979) observed that children go through two stages of play when faced with new material or equipment. First they engaged in a period of epistemic play, followed by ludic play:

1 *Epistemic play*: Here the child considers – What is this? What does this do? as a new material or piece of equipment is investigated and possibilities searched for. In Figure 5.1 a 2-year-old boy is exploring the properties of a 'down puff'.
2 *Ludic play*: When the child wonders – How can I use it? This occurs when the child knows about the material or equipment and is practising his/her skills.

To deepen and develop their understanding of material and equipment children need to be able to use all their senses.

Exploring and developing mastery of ideas

The theories of McKellar (1957) and others, give us an insight into the creative process at work in our thinking. During this process we need to

---

Example

At the age of 18 months Samuel, Damian and Dean were introduced to paint by Kim and Lydia, the nursery officers in the toddler room. The room was carefully prepared so that the children would have the opportunity to explore the new material freely. Tables and chairs were removed, the walls and floor covered with lining paper and bowls of paint in primary colours were laid out on the floor. The children were also carefully prepared! Clothes were removed and baths of warm water were ready to bathe the children when they had finished.

At first the children were tentative and looked to the adults for reassurance that the paint was available for them to use freely. First fingers, then hands were placed in the paint, the paint was smelt and tasted as well as touched and looked at. The children used their hands and feet to explore. They discovered that the paint made marks and that the movements they made with their hands or feet influenced the mark on the paper.

From time to time the children would look at the adults for reassurance and Kim and Lydia would indicate their approval. By the end of the session the children had mastered new skills and concepts related to paint. They knew some of the properties of paint, for example, that it dripped and could be used to make a variety of lines and shapes. They were becoming aware that when they mixed two colours together a change took place and a new colour was created.

By the end of the session their ability to control the paint and the marks it made had increased. The adults had left the children to explore the paint safely. Each child had made their own discoveries and learnt by watching the other children present.

---

saturate ourselves with ideas, to become so familiar with the concepts involved in the particular problem that we are solving that we can recall them automatically.

When people are exploring a problem or developing mastery of a new piece of information they appear to go through a number of stages. They:

- become aware of a problem, a new idea or pieces of information
- start to tackle the problem by brainstorming ideas and using their existing knowledge and understanding to identify connections, similarities and differences
- ponder and allow the idea to incubate. This may take place over a number of days or minutes
- have an insight into the problem, a moment of illumination that helps them to understand the problem or the new piece of information

Figure 5.1 Philip, aged 2 years 4 months exploring the texture of a 'down puff'.

- identify a possible solution, establish a meaningful connection and become aware of a solution. This is the moment of creativity
- test the solution or understanding of the idea for themselves or with others which may lead them to modify their solution or understanding.

This process is similar to Piaget's idea of disequilibrium, when thinking has to change to incorporate new information. It is this process that moves children through the stages of development we discussed in the last chapter. Children's interpretation of the world is challenged when they take on the new information and find that they now have two contradictory views of the same event. This causes them to question their view-point and raises doubts about which interpretation is the correct one, which in turn results in cognitive disequilibrium. This sense of unease motivates them to change their thinking to accommodate the new perspective.

When we are involved in exploring new ideas, the process we engage in is both conscious and unconscious. It requires what McKellar calls 'receptivity', the ability to be receptive to what others have done before and to information gained through our own perceptions (McKellar 1957). During the process we move backward and forward in our thinking – it is not a linear approach. The whole process may take days or minutes. Frequently, our solution or grasp of an idea will lead us on to a new idea or problem – a new challenge to overcome.

A *model of the creative process in young children*

Though Hutt's work concentrates on the creative process as it relates to children's mastery of equipment and materials, and McKellar focuses on exploring ideas, there are many similarities in the processes they describe. Cecil et al. (1985) offer us a model of the creative process that pulls together the ideas of Hutt and McKellar. They show how the ideas of each of these writers relate to each other and bring them together to provide a complete process. Their model can be used to support the creative process whether it relates to ideas or equipment or a combination of both. It provides us with a model that we can use in our work with children. There are four levels in this process:

1 *Curiosity* – or what is it? Children are alert, interested and want to know more. Their attention has been taken.
2 *Exploration* – or what can and does it do? Children can be observed actively investigating objects, events or ideas. They are often using all their senses to gather information. Watching others can also be part of their investigation
3 *Play* – or what can I do with this? Children initiate a period of total immersion characterized by spontaneity and often without clear final objectives. As there is little or no focus on a predetermined product they are free to examine all kinds of detail during this period that they may have missed if they had been concentrating on the end product. This is an opportunity to practise and consolidate the skills and knowledge they have acquired in the earlier levels.
4 *Creativity* – or what can I create or invent? The child discovers uncommon or new approaches to the materials or problem they are investigating, they take risks and make new connections.

These levels overlap and evolve out of each other. The process may take place over a period of a few hours or over many days (see Figure 5.2).

The *importance of errors*

The creative process is characterized by risk-taking, trying things out and experimenting. For every truly creative act there will be many that did not

Figure 5.2   Curiosity, exploration and play overlap as Amina, 2 years 2 months, discovers the possibilities inherent in a variety of musical instruments.

succeed, where the ideas or materials connected did not work. These apparent failures are crucial to the creative process. If children know the result already they are not engaging their creativity, or are not discovering something new to them. It is at the point when children discover that something they thought would work does not; or that a guess was not correct, that they find out something they had not realized before and understanding moves on. This allows them to refine their approach to the problem or material under investigation. Children have the ability to work things out and develop their thinking by themselves. Errors are important because they move thinking forward. They are thus vital to the creative process.

If children are to feel free to make mistakes they need to be in control of the creative process. They need to know that the adults around them understand the importance of pursuing seemingly irrational ideas. When

---

Example

The children at Dorothy Gardner, aged between 1 and 5 years, had been exploring hand drums as part of an investigation of the music associated with celebration. This led on to an interest in drum kits and Stan, a drummer, brought his kit to show the children. This was the first time that most of them had seen a drum kit at such close range and had the opportunity to play it. The initial reaction was curiosity, the children looked and touched the different drums, the cymbals, the sticks and beaters. They asked Stan questions – what were the names of the different parts of the kit? How did he play them? What was the hole in the bass drum for? How did he carry so many drums and cymbals? He showed them how he got a range of sounds from the kit and how he used his hands and feet together to produce rhythms. The children then explored the kit themselves. They tried different sticks, brushes and beaters and found out how they sounded on the different drums, they varied the force with which they hit the drums, they used their hands to feel the vibrations made when the drums and cymbals were hit. As the children became more confident they played with the skills and knowledge they had acquired, practising and perfecting them. For the youngest children the thrill of getting an impressively loud sound was the culmination of the process. The older children created their own rhythms and patterns, some spent the whole session perfecting a particular rhythm, only stopping when it was time for Stan to leave. The way in which different children used the drums varied, sometimes according to age and skill, sometimes according to personality and interest. For some children the process halted at the exploration or play stage, but others went on to create their own patterns and rhythms or represent their experience through drawings.

---

children are making errors they are operating at the limits of their abilities, whether cognitive or physical, and are stretching themselves. Or as my husband says to his drum students 'if you're not making mistakes, you're not trying hard enough!'

Schema

Children's behaviour reflects their growing interest in the world around them – the physical world, the people in it and their relationships to the child. Sometimes children seem to become interested in patterns of behaviour that appear to be random, pointless and sometimes downright annoying. For instance, they continually throw things, or take objects from one place to another or spend long periods of time wrapping articles up. But Athey (1990) helps us to see these behaviours in a different light.

Athey looked at commonalities and continuities in young children's thoughts and behaviour. She identified patterns of repeatable behaviour that young children engage in, and offers us an insight into their function for the child and the process involved. Drawing on Piaget's work, Athey called these repeatable patterns of behaviour schema and argues that they are crucial to learning as they enable the child to focus on a particular concept and explore it in depth.

When children are involved in a schema they are engaged in a creative process, as they are making new connections and reaching new understandings. Among the common, repeatable patterns of behaviour that Athey and others have observed are schema of:

- *Rotation*: an interest in things that turn. For example, wheels, cogs
- *Enclosure*: an interest in enclosing spaces. For example, drawing closed shapes, building barricades
- *Enveloping*: an interest in completely covering objects or space, for example, wrapping parcels, wrapping up in blankets
- *Trajectory*: an interest in objects and people moving or flying through the air. For example, planes, rockets, leaping, throwing
- *Transporting*: an interest in moving objects or collections of any kind from one area to another, for example, using a bag or truck to move blocks from one corner of the room to another
- *Connecting*: an interest in fastening or joining things together, for example, connecting railway carriages and train tracks, tying knots.

(Nicholls 1986)

Children's involvement in a particular schema is demonstrated by their repeated interest in aspects of the physical world which demonstrate these elements and in forms of representation which allow them to explore their current schema.

Conclusion

There is a fine balance between ensuring that children are offered materials, equipment, ideas and experiences that are challenging, but not so far removed from the children's existing experiences and knowledge that they are perceived as threatening. The degree of novelty needed to stimulate investigation needs to be just right. Too much newness in the

---

Example

Nina, aged 2, became captivated by rotation. At home her mother reported her fascination with the tumble dryer, rotating microwave tray and washing machine, 'Round and round the garden' was her favourite song. Meal times became more exciting, if slightly messier, by Nina's discovery that plates and bowls could be made to spin! At nursery the space in the garden enabled her to experiment and represent her schema with larger body movement. She could spin until dizzy and fall down safely on the safety surface, she could rotate on the roundabout and was particularly delighted by the way her clothes and hair spun out as she went round. Her drawings during this period mirrored her absorption. Using as many different colours as possible she built up layers of spirals and circles.

---

experiences we offer can lead to children becoming anxious as they are unable to link the new experience to their existing frameworks. The link between the creative process and security is strong. If we get the balance wrong and children feel insecure and uncertain they will cease to explore, and the result may be avoidance rather than creativity! Yet if the experience, material or situation offered is too familiar it offers no challenge and can lead to the child ignoring it rather than becoming involved.

The role we adopt, the environment we create, the way we present experiences and materials are all crucial in ensuring that this balance is right. In the next few chapters we will be looking at ways in which we can achieve this:

- *Chapter 6*: What are the roles adults need to undertake?
- *Chapter 7*: How do we organize the environment to encourage creativity and imagination?
- *Chapter 8*: in what ways can we extend children's experiences?
- *Chapter 9*: How can we assess, record and plan children's creative and imaginative development?

Summary

This chapter has:

- stressed the importance of knowing the process involved in creativity

- suggested that the first stage is mastery of equipment, materials and ideas

- suggested that the second stage is using these for our own creative purposes
- emphasized the importance of errors
- looked briefly at schema.

Further reading

Athey, C. (1990) *Extending Thought in Young Children: A Parent–Teacher Partnership.* London: Paul Chapman.
   Athey analyses over 5000 observations of children and provides positive interpretations of a wide range of children's behaviour.
Cecil, L. M., Gray, M. M., Thornbug, K. R. and Ispa, J. (1985) Curiosity-exploration-play: the early childhood mosaic. *Early Child Development and Care,* 19: 199–217.
   This article describes the background to the model referred to in this chapter.
Hutt, C. (1979) 'Play in the under fives: form, development, and function', in J. G. Howells (ed.) *Modern Perspectives in the Psychiatry of Infancy.* New York: Bruner Marcel.
   Hutt explains her ideas on children's play.
McKellar, P. (1957) *Imagination and Thinking.* London: Cohen and West.
   Chapter 8 looks at the conditions of creativity and the creative process.

Things to think about

- Can you identify examples of the creative process in your own life?

- How do you feel when you are disturbed when engaged in this process?

- How do you feel when you make a new discovery?

- Do you want to share this with others?

Part Three

Theory into practice

One never notices what has been done, one only sees what remains to be done.

Marie Curie

6

The role of the adult

Introduction

This chapter will look at:

- how adults can foster creative and imaginative development
- the range of roles adults undertake
- the non-interventionist role
- the interventionist role
- intervening with sensitivity
- creating conditions which inspire children
- developing creativity and imagination through our interactions with children
- the role of the adult in each area
- the role of the adult at different stages of development.

How adults can foster creative and imaginative development

Adults' attitudes are crucial to the development of creativity and imagination in young children. If we do not create an atmosphere that values these areas of learning and development children will not respond. But what exactly is our role?

- Should we become directly involved or would this stifle children's natural creativity?
- Should we provide the equipment and materials and stand back or would this result in a lack of progress and challenge?
- How do we balance the danger of over-direction against anxieties about becoming involved?

Often our own early childhood experiences and influences can hinder us. We may have been told that we were no good at art or music. We may have been made to feel ungainly by an insensitive dance teacher (I was told by one that I moved like a clumsy elephant!) or as my brother was told, that he had 'no imagination'. The embarrassment, anxieties and fears that these responses to our early creative and imaginative representations make, can re-surface in later life. Do we have the ability to support young children's creative and imaginative development? In this chapter we will be looking at these issues and hopefully finding some reassuring answers.

The range of roles adults undertake

Supporting and promoting young children's creativity and imagination involves us in a number of roles. We may be the child's parent or an educator who is not part of the family. These different roles have different characteristics. Parents are, quite rightly, biased in favour of their children, while educators, who are not part of the family can take on a more objective role and introduce children to the expectations of a wider world. Parents are 'experts' on their own child, while other educators are experts on children at a particular age and stage of development. By each bringing their own perspectives and expertise together, we can provide the best for each child. Views differ on the roles adults should undertake when they are supporting young children's creativity and imagination. For simplicity we will divide these into two approaches:

1 *Non-interventionist*: those who think that adults should not become directly involved in young children's creative and imaginative work.
2 *Interventionist*: those who believe that the interaction between children and adult are keys to children's learning and development.

A *non-interventionist role*

The history of art education offers insights into the changing views on the adult role in encouraging creativity. Pickering (1976) explains that in the last century children were viewed as inept artists who needed to be taught the skills and techniques that would enable them to produce art work that met adult expectations and purposes. One has only to look at the carefully crafted samplers produced by girls from a relatively young age to see this approach in action.

The work of art educators such as Cizek (Viola 1937) and Richardson (1948), challenged this view and led to a change in attitude. They believed that:

- children were artists in their own right who should not be forced or pressed to produce images to meet adult expectations
- children's self-expression was important.

These views have led to a concern that by intervening in children's creative and imaginative processes adults may harm or even destroy children's natural creativity by imposing on them adult views and preconceptions. If we intervene with a view that the purpose of art is to produce an image that is as realistic as possible and therefore think of children as failed realists we may do great harm by imposing inappropriate expectations which do not match children's developmental stage.

Adults are also fearful, sometimes with justification, that their involvement with children's imaginative play means taking it over and imposing on children's imaginative processes. Some of the models of adult involvement used in play tutoring have developed from a view that children's imaginative play is deficient in some way. As we saw in Chapter 3, there can be cultural and religious reasons why children's engagement in imaginative play differs.

Another influence for those who advocate a 'hands off' approach has been Piaget's views on children's development. As we saw in Chapter 4, Piaget identified stages in child development. For him, creativity is an aspect of cognition and so relies on children's intellectual level. During the early stages of development, young children do not yet think logically and are therefore unable to see different spatial and social viewpoints. For Piaget, children were rooted in immediate perception. Progression from one stage to the next was the result of children's efforts to assimilate and accommodate new experiences. Development was largely unaffected by the interventions of adults in the process, learning followed development and development was dependent on the child's pace and could not be influenced by adults. Piaget's influence has sometimes led to the view that the adult's role is supervisory rather than interactive. The adult's role is to provide a stimulating environment and to identify the stage of development individual children have reached so that appropriate materials can be presented, rather than to actively intervene in the learning process.

An interventionist role

However, as we saw earlier, children are born with the desire to communicate with others. Piaget failed to understand the importance of this. Human beings are essentially cooperative. We want to share our thoughts and feelings, and to do this we need physical actions, language and symbols. Meanings are established by communicating with each other, sharing thoughts and emotions through a range of representations (Trevarthen 1995). Young children want to share their creative and imaginative representations with adults and adults can help them increase their ability to communicate their thoughts, feelings and ideas through their representations.

Piaget's views led him to undervalue the role of the adult. There is a danger that children are not presented with challenging experiences because they are not deemed ready to understand them. Before new experiences can be presented, children must be perceived as ready.

Vygotsky (1978) offers us an alternative model. Unlike Piaget, he stresses the importance of the social context – what children can do with other people. In Vygotsky's view, Piaget's work has led to a tendency to focus on what children can do unaided, what they already know or can do. Too often learning is directed at yesterday's development. For Vygotsky, development is dependent on learning. It is through learning that children develop. Learning should be matched to the child's level of development but should also take them beyond it (see Figure 6.1 – 'Scaffolding' is explained below).

Through his observations of young children, he identified a period in which children need assistance to complete a task. This fell between two levels of development:

1 *The children's actual level of development*: this is a completed development cycle, when children understand a concept, skill, or idea, and can use it on their own.
2 *Potential level of development*: this is the level the children can achieve if supported by a competent learner.

The distance between the actual level of development and potential level of development is the 'zone of proximal development'. Experiences and teaching targeted at this zone will best support the children's learning.

Figure 6.1 A key worker scaffolds the learning of a group of 3- and 4-year-olds as they work with dough.

These are the functions that have not yet been mastered but are in the process of being mastered. This is where the adult should focus. Children need to interact with other people if their learning is to progress. Once children have internalized a concept, skill or idea and are able to use it by themselves, without the assistance of a competent learner, it becomes their actual level of development.

Bruner (1975) built on Vygotsky's ideas and introduced the concept of 'scaffolding' children's learning from his observations of the way in which parents interact with their children and especially their role in language development. His observations led him to the hypothesis that parent's are extremely skilled at supporting their children's learning by providing a 'scaffold' based on their intimate knowledge of the child. But what is natural and spontaneous between the parent and child needs to be made conscious when we are working with children who are not our own.

Children construct knowledge and add new information to what is already known. When they are presented with new information, children look for similarities and differences to find ways to attach it to existing knowledge. Sometimes they need to deconstruct aspects of their understanding in order to incorporate the new knowledge. While children are engaged in this process they need ways of holding experiences together.

They need a scaffold. The adult's role is to provide this scaffold. When scaffolding children's learning adults need to be:

- finely tuned to the children's ability
- provide a flexible framework and be aware of where children may be heading
- respond to and follow up remarks and comment from children.

Cox (1992) has criticized some of the approaches to art education that have developed from the work of Cizek and Richardson. She argues against approaches which are based on the view that development and learning take care of themselves. While children may produce representations that delight the adult eye by their free use of materials as a result of these approaches, they do not necessarily deepen children's understanding. When adults are unclear about how or when to aid children they tend to indiscriminately label everything as 'good'. The result can be a strategy that is so 'hands off' that it leaves children without the skills and knowledge to progress, the consequence being that they become frustrated, and develop an image of themselves as being no good at the performing and visual arts. Too often we hear older children and adults say 'I'm no good at art or music. I can't draw or sing.' Their initial delight in drawing, construction, painting, music-making and role play changes to reluctance and uncertainty.

Kindler (1995) observed children in her son's day-care centre. She found that though the area was well supplied with a variety of materials the children took little advantage of them. Only when adults were physically present in the area and became involved with the children did the children's participation, concentration and exploration increase. Her conclusion was that the mere availability of materials is not enough, adult input is essential.

In imaginative play, sensitive adult involvement can support children by helping them to focus on the narrative they are developing and increasing the complexity of the scenarios they are acting out.

Intervening with sensitivity

We are social beings, born with the need to represent and communicate our experiences. Through our interactions with others we grow and develop and our role as adults is to ensure that the children for whom we are responsible have this opportunity. The key is to know individual children and groups of children well. Interventions should support and extend children's learning and development by adding the information or skill they need at the point they need it. Interventions that are based on the view that children are failed realists or deficient in imaginative play skills are unhelpful, and undervalue young children's considerable creative and imaginative expertise. We need to intervene with sensitivity. Our role is to:

- create conditions within which children are inspired to be creative and imaginative
- develop children's creativity and imagination through our interactions with them

Creating conditions which inspire children

As adults we need to:

- be aware of the nature and value of creativity and imagination
- be knowledgeable about:
  - the development and process involved
  - the range of experiences to be provided
  - the role of the adult in each area of representation (see Table 6.1)
  - the role of the adult at different stages of development (see Table 6.2)
  - probable patterns of interest
- be aware of the importance of equal opportunities and the need for equality by ensuring that the environment, experiences and activities provided are:
  - equally inviting to children from a range of cultures
  - appealing to girls and boys
  - suitable for those with special needs
- be honest about their personal prejudices and challenge their own assumptions
- value each child's representations as unique and personal to her or him
- plan the physical environment:
  - does the environment feed the child's imagination and stimulate their creativity?
  - is the environment exciting and aesthetically pleasing? (if not, see Chapter 7!)
- plan, observe, record and assess the children's use of the environment and experiences (see Chapter 8)
- ensure that there is time and space for the child to work alone, as well as with groups of children and with adults (see Figure 6.2)
- deploy the available adults in the most effective way and encourage the children to use adults as a resource

Table 6.1 The specific adult role in each area

Two- and three-dimensional representation	Music and dance	Imaginative play
• drawing, painting, sculpting alongside the children • demonstrating new materials, equipment and techniques • introducing artists and crafts people to the children • arranging visits to galleries and studios • providing sufficient space to work, especially for block play • providing space and protection for work in progress • ensuring there is space to display work and time to reflect and comment on it adult to child and child to child	• dancing and making music alongside the children • demonstrating new instruments • ensuring there is sufficient space to dance freely • introducing musicians and dancers to the children • arranging visits to see live performance • providing sufficient instruments for group playing • recording dance and music through photographs, videos and audio cassettes to enable children to look back and comment on their representations	• suggesting actions to children • threading together a sequence of actions • supporting children in entering play and signalling to others a wish to become involved • helping children to move from one action to another to develop narrative • encouraging children who don't get involved • helping older children to act out story for example, fairy tale – as fantasy play is further removed from the child's first-hand experience it is harder to maintain • providing environment which encourages full range of roles and range of plans

Table 6.2 The specific adult role at each stage of development

The adult supports by:

Birth–1 year
- recognizing the importance of repeating actions and sounds, imitating expressions, actions and sounds for the baby to copy
- encouraging babies from 6 months onwards to move from a passive role to a more active, initiating role and responding to them
- using changing, feeding and bathing times as opportunities to support the baby's curiosity by interacting with them
- providing opportunities to explore objects and sounds by bringing them within the baby's sight and reach, for example, mobiles
- providing opportunities for the baby to explore everyday objects in an accessible way, for example, in baskets
- talking with the baby about what they see and responding to their utterances

1–2 years
- extending the length of the play episode and offering a commentary to the child
- providing room, space and time to explore *safely*
- providing a wider range and quantity of materials which offer plenty of opportunities for exploring what materials will do
- providing opportunities for exploratory play
- supporting emerging schema, for example, transporting, enveloping, heaping, collecting, fitting into and through.
- providing opportunities to explore inside and outside, trips to shops and parks, short journeys on public transport
- being attentive and thereby increasing the learning potential of the experiences offered
- offering children a commentary on their actions and gradually increasing the complexity of the language used
- encouraging role play, copying what the adults around them do is important, for example, pretending to cook using dough

Table 6.2 Continued

	The adult supports by:
2–3 years	• providing security when new people or experiences are encountered • providing the companionship of other children who become increasingly important as partners in children's play • helping children to build relationships with a wider range of adults who offer new roles to imitate and explore • supporting children's interest in representing their experiences of a widening world by access to a variety of materials and toys • enabling children to choose the experience that matches their interest and needs
3–4 years	• organizing the day to allow sufficient time for child-initiated activities and experiences • ensuring that children have the skills they need to match the representations they wish to make as their wishes become more complex • introducing children to the work of others across culture and through ages and developing critical abilities
4–5 years	• ensuring props are available for fantasy play • supporting and encouraging the use of unrealistic props for imaginative play • helping the children to increase the complexity of the narratives they act, for example, through asking questions about what happened next and the characters' motivations • introducing standard notation
6 years	• ensuring that there is still sufficient time for self-initiated activity as curriculum demands increase • encouraging children to work together to produce more complex representations than they can achieve alone • ensuring that children have a love of the visual and performing arts that will stay with them throughout life

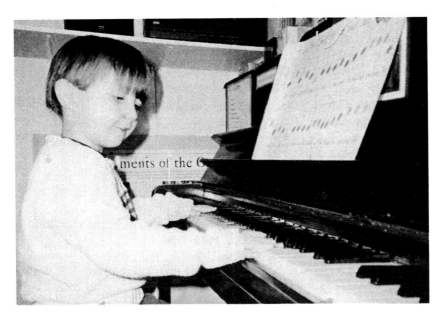

Figure 6.2 We need to ensure that there is time and space to work alone. Felix, aged 3 years 7 months, spent the morning by himself at the piano creating music based on the sounds of the church organ he had heard the day before.

- communicate with parents and others to ensure that:
  - they build on the children's creative and imaginative experiences in the home and community
  - the parents of children are informed of their creative and imaginative experiences
  - parents are involved and influence the setting
- provide access to artists, crafts people, musicians, dancers
- act as researcher:
  - analysing research and it implications for our practice
  - analysing our own practice and modifying as necessary
  - discussing our work with others.

Developing children's creativity and imagination through our interactions with them

As adults we need to:

- be empathetic, that is, seeing the world through the eyes of the children
- offer children secure relationships which allow curiosity to flourish
- be facilitators enabling the children to (see Figure 6.1):

- use their own abilities to the full and acquire new skills
- understand the process involved in creative and imaginative experiences
- find their own voice and style, not simply to imitate others
- be in control of representations they create
- detect and identify possibilities within materials
- discriminate and be critical of their own and others' work
- recognize that the process may be more important than the product on some occasions
- demonstrate the use of new materials and equipment to children
- value children's self-initiated activity and representations by being available, interested and involved with the children
- recognize the importance of knowing when to be silent, when to encourage, when to inspire and when to help
- offer a model of a more experienced learner or of creative and imaginative behaviour by working alongside children as a partner
- establish with the children clear guiding principles, such as rules for use of materials and acceptable behaviour
- extend children's knowledge and skills through encouraging critical reflection and offering feedback

---

Example

At 1 year 9 months Michael became passionate about mechanical diggers. According to his father this started on a trip to the local park when Michael spotted a digger. He spent some time observing the machine, watching how it moved and the effect it had on the earth. His interest was infectious and the workmen operating the machine stopped to enable him to take a closer look. They showed him the different parts of the machine and let him look in the cab. On his return home Michael demanded that his father draw him a picture of the digger and the 'diggermen'. His parents took his interests seriously and during the next few weeks helped to search out pictures of diggers in books and posters. They answered his questions about diggers and made time to look at diggers and other vehicles when they went out. Michael drew pictures of diggers with diggermen, built up his collection of toy diggers and communicated his passion to any adult who visited! Anyone visiting the house was asked to add to his collection of digger drawings and Michael watched carefully as they drew correcting any mistakes they made. He used his collection to act out stories involving diggers. Michael had become, with the support of his parents, an expert on diggers and their representation.

Example

Sioban, aged 4 years 11 months, and Louis, aged 3 years 10 months, were in the construction area using the large blocks. Susan, a member of staff, was in the home corner nearby with two other children.

Sioban: Susan, Susan I've made Rama and Sita's horse!

Susan: Oh, wow!

Sioban: Yes! Yes! That's when Rama rescues Sita and they fly away.

Susan: And what happens next?

Sioban: Me and Louis are going to make the wedding.

Louis: And me. And me, I'm Rama!

Susan: What do you need? [*The exchange continues as props are identified and the children are helped by the adult to prepare for the wedding.*]

- present activities and experiences which emphasize exploration and active participation on the part of the children
- establish interactions which emphasize the role of adult and children learning together
- be genuine and honest. Praising every child's every representation is not being honest, but offering constructive feedback and encouragement is
- discuss children's representation with them. Help them to talk about how their representations work, the elements of art, music, dance they have used and the feelings induced
- help them make connections with the work of others

Example – A cautionary tale!

Shayma, age 5, was working in the graphics area, engrossed in her drawing. When she finished Shayma came over to me, holding her drawing behind her back.

Shayma: I want to show you something.

Me: Oh, let me see, show me.

Shayma: *But* only show you if you promise not to ask me to tell you about it.

Me: What do you mean?

Shayma: Every time I show you something you say 'Oh it's lovely, do tell me about it!' Sometimes I just want to show you my drawings, not tell you about them, sometimes they're for looking at.

- pause before speaking and give children the opportunity to communicate their view of their work first. Do not assume that the adult interpretation is the correct one
- give children time to respond to questions and comments made by adults and other children
- recognize the importance of verbal and non-verbal communication in adults and children. Does your posture, expression, tone of voice and eye contact indicate interest or boredom?

Conclusion

Children do not require us to be perfect but they do require us to be committed. There will always be a conflict between our ideals and reality, between what we want to provide for children and the realities of our situation. We can easily become despondent and feel that there is little we can do. We can feel that the environment we find ourselves in is unsuitable and unsympathetic, or that we are not skilled enough. Whether we see this gap as failure or a challenge is up to us. But if we adopt an attitude of failure we fail ourselves and the children.

In our work with children we adopt a variety of roles. Perhaps the most crucial are:

- relationships which encourage security and trust
- models of the creative process in action in our own lives.

Summary

This chapter has established that:

- adults are crucial to children's development in creativity and imagination

- adults need to be aware of the variety of roles they have and find ways to accomplish them

- concerns about intruding on children' representations need to be addressed but

- we must also be aware of the importance of adult–child interactions in learning and development

- we need to create an environment where adults and children are learning together.

Further reading

Bruner, J. (1975) The ontogenesis of speech acts. *Journal of Child Language*, 2: 1–9.
   Bruner discusses the concept of 'scaffolding'.
Cox, M. (1992) *Children's Drawings*. London: Penguin.
   Cox argues that drawing is a demanding skill with its own set of techniques.
Kindler, A. (1995) 'Significance of adult input in early childhood artistic develop-
   ment', in C. M. Thompson (ed.) *The Visual Arts and Early Childhood*. Washington,
   DC: National Association for the Education of Children.
   Kindler discusses the role of the adult and the necessity of adult input.
Pickering, J. (1976) 'Visual education for young children', in D. Brothwell (ed.)
   Beyond Aesthetics: Investigations into the Nature of Visual Art. London: Thames and
   Hudson.
   Pickering looks at the changes that art education has experienced since its emer-
   gence in the 19th century.
Vygotsky, L. (1978) *Mind in Society*. Cambridge, Mass.: Harvard University Press.
   Chapter 6 looks at the relationship between learning and development.

Things to think about

- How would you describe your view of your role?

- Are there any aspects of your role that you do not feel confident about?

- What can you do to build your own confidence?

7

The organization of space, time and social contexts

Introduction

This chapter will look at:

- why the right environment is important
- how the physical space can encourage creativity and imagination
- how we use the time available to promote creativity and imagination
- how we can deploy available adults
- the importance of peers and opportunities to share with others in creative and imaginative experiences.

Why the right environment is important

If we want children to express their creativity we need to provide an environment in which they can do this. There are two aspects we need to bear in mind:

1 the emotional environment we create
2 the physical environment we create.

In previous chapters we have looked at the importance of adult attitudes in the promotion of creativity and imagination. These attitudes create the emotional environment. If we wish children to be creative we need to ensure that all children feel valued and accepted for themselves and their culture, religion or language group. Without this children will not feel sufficiently secure to take risks or make mistakes and these, as we saw in Chapter 5, are crucial in the creative process.

Increasingly, children's opportunities to explore freely are being curtailed. Parents' concerns about safety may mean that children are no longer able to play freely in streets or parks unless they are closely supervised by adults. To compensate for the decrease in children's free play opportunities there has been an increase in organized activity for children. Children often attend a variety of dance, music and drama groups from a young age. These are frequently adult-directed and do not allow children the time and space to explore and create in their own ways. We need to find ways to reverse this trend and ensure that in the environments we create for children they do have the opportunities they need.

Organization of and access to space and resource

The way in which we organize and use the available space inside and out is crucial in creating opportunities for children to express their creativity. Children need sufficient space to work and easily accessible resources if they are to make the best use of creative and imaginative experiences offered to them. The space will vary greatly. It may be in a home or in a centre-based setting. Each setting will offer its own possibilities. For example, it can be easier to create the sense of security that encourages creativity in a home-based setting, which is familiar to children, than in centre-based settings which can feel large and institutional. On the other hand, those in centre-based settings may be fortunate in having purpose-built premises set aside for their sole use and designed with easy access to resources and the space for children to engage in a wide variety of creative and imaginative experiences. We need to look at each setting and maximize its potential for creativity and imagination.

To some degree creativity is resource-led. Without access to resources it is hard for children to demonstrate their creativity, especially when trying to create two- and three-dimensional representations. The range of resources and organization we provide will determine what and how the children can create and how creative they can be. Creativity is about making meaningful connections, using ideas and/or materials in new ways. Our organization of space and resources will largely determine whether children can do this.

While space and resources will vary between settings it is important that whatever is available is organized in a tidy way. It is frustrating for children and adults if they are delayed and possibly distracted by being unable to find a resource or piece of equipment at a crucial moment. Examination of the work areas of artists and crafts people often reveals well-organized space where everything is easy to locate and readily at hand. McKellar (1957) explains that the arrangement of the physical space can aid concentration, create a mood conducive to creativity and increase motivation.

Children's access to creative and imaginative experiences can be limited for a number of reasons, some valid, others less so. Lack of space and time, an unsympathetic caretaker or cleaner, adults' degree of tolerance about mess, adults' lack of understanding about the importance of these experiences – all can have a major impact on creativity and imagination. For example, parents and other carers looking after children at home may have limited space and resources available to them compared with centre-based settings. It may not be possible to offer as wide a range of experiences all the time, but the smaller number of children involved makes it possible to concentrate on the particular experiences that are engaging the children at any given time. Kitchen tables and floors provide surfaces to work on, blankets draped over tables and chairs provide a private space for children to reflect in and the everyday items and familiar routines of home-life present excellent opportunities for imaginative play. The example in the introduction shows that a domestic setting is just as likely to encourage imagination as a purpose-built centre filled with resources.

The following examples show how staff in centre-based settings adapted their environment to meet the creative and imaginative needs of children.

Tables 7.1–7.4 are designed to help you to audit your environment. If you find gaps ask yourself if they are there for a valid reason or is there something that you can do to increase children's access?

- *Table 7.1* is for auditing the general environment
- *Table 7.2* is for auditing the environment for two- and three-dimensional representations
- *Table 7.3* is for auditing the environment for music and dance representations
- *Table 7.4* is for auditing the environment for imaginative play.

Care of equipment and resources

The equipment and materials the children use and have access to needs to be well cared for and used safely. For example, clay needs to be stored in a way that ensures that it is damp but not sodden. It should not be left in contact with paper and other materials, which will rot and make the

---

Example

A staff group became concerned by the children's low interest in and
use of the area of the nursery set aside for music and dance. The area
was well stocked with a range of musical instruments that were well
labelled and easy for the children to access. Despite this, observations
of the children revealed that they rarely used the area for music and
never for dance. Children who did use the area only stayed for a
matter of minutes and seemed to be using the piano stool as a resting
place between activities! They observed that the area was next to the
book corner, listening area and the large construction area as well as
near a passageway to the garden door. Proximity to the book and
listening areas meant that children were not free to explore sound as
this disturbed children who were reading. While in theory there was
space to dance and move, the nearness to the construction area meant
that this space got taken over by the large hollow blocks. Being on the
route to the door was distracting. A discussion at a staff meeting
reached the conclusion that the music and dance area was badly
positioned. If the children were to explore music and dance freely, they
needed to re-allocate and reorganize the available space. After a great
deal of discussion, argument and compromise, an alternative space
was identified. Further observation of the children revealed higher
levels of concentration, increased complexity in dance and movement
and creative use of the musical instruments.

---

clay smelly. It is preferable to use hessian rather than newspaper to roll
and prepare clay for use. The clay dust can be harmful and care needs to
be taken to reduce any dust. Scissors, saws and other cutting equipment
need to be kept sharp and clean. Blunt instruments mean undue pressure
which leads to accidents. Make sure that you know how to store and prepare the equipment and materials the children will be using.

There is the potential for any equipment to be used inappropriately and
possibly harmfully. To avoid accident or mishap, and create an environment that is conducive to creativity, we need to ensure that the children:

- know how to use equipment and material in the correct way
- show an awareness of the need for self-discipline and respect for others
- are aware of the importance of behaving appropriately to ensure their
  own safety and the safety of others, for example, they should not run or
  move carelessly while holding sharp objects such as scissors.

While there are common rules, each setting will also have its own

Example

Staff in a group for carers and young children wanted to create a space in their room specifically for babies. The room available was used by a large group of 0–3-year-olds and their parents and carers. Staff were concerned that babies did not have as many opportunities to explore and discover as the older children. In consultation with parents and carers, they organized the space and resources to maximize the opportunities for creative explorations. They did this by:

- ensuring that the area was sufficiently enclosed so that the babies could explore without disruptions from more mobile children
- organizing the resources in a way that was accessible to babies who were not yet mobile. For example, by organizing resources in treasure baskets (Goldschmied and Jackson 1994) hanging objects from string within reach of the babies as they sat, organizing tins and boxes on low shelves for babies who were starting to crawl
- providing materials and objects that stimulated all the senses. For example, mirrors at babies' height on the wall for babies to watch their own expressions and those of others, reflective strips of paper hanging from the ceiling to catch the light, lemons and oranges in the treasure baskets to smell and taste, bells hanging from string to shake, sealed plastic bottles containing seeds and pulses to rattle, lengths of fabric attached to the wall to feel and stroke.

The babies responded to the environment with enthusiasm. Staff and parents observed them spending up to forty-five minutes exploring the resources available, often in the company of another child (see Figure 7.1).

individual rules based on particular circumstances. It is important that an appropriate balance is ensured between safety and the freedom to experiment with resources and ideas. Adults need to make sure that the rules in use are genuinely to do with safety and respect for others and not to do with their own prejudice, bias or convenience!

Organizing time to promote creativity and imagination

As we saw in Chapter 5 the creative process takes time. We need time to experiment and explore, to play and practise, to try new ideas and modify our representations in response to the feedback we get. This means that we

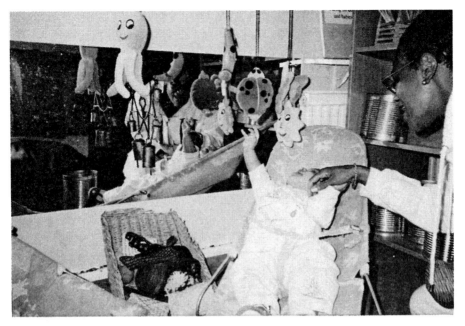

Figure 7.1 Bernice, aged 5 months exploring an environment created to stimulate the baby's creativity and imagination.

need to think about the organization of the time available to ensure that the children have as much of it as possible to engage in creative and imaginative experiences.

As children grow older it can seem that much of the school day is taken up with the core subjects, and that creativity and imagination are seen as a luxury or extra to be fitted in when the core curriculum has been delivered. But in Chapters 1 and 2 we saw how important creativity and imagination are for all areas of learning and that through creative experiences children's learning in the core areas can be enhanced. A cross-curricular approach allows us to draw on the appeal and potential of creative experiences to encourage learning and development in all areas of the curriculum.

Whatever the circumstance or restraints we work under, we need to look at the time available and make sure that it is put to the best use:

- Is the session organized in a way that allows for uninterrupted exploration and does it minimize interruptions?
- Is there an appropriate balance between child- and adult-initiated activity?

Table 7.1 What does the environment you offer provide?

Feature	Questions	Yes/No	What do we need to improve?
Space	• are there opportunities for children to move and think with bodies? • are there opportunities to work inside and out? • are there areas to be active, to work alone or with others? • are there areas for reflection and contemplation? • can children leave work that is under construction and return to it later? • is there space for storing and displaying a range of equipment and resources? For example, at home by using portable boxes for resources • is the space organized in a way that is practical and manageable? • is it tidy, is there a place for everything and is it clearly labelled? • are materials organized in a way that enable children to combine them in new and creative ways? • is the outside space used in a way that complements the inside, for example, by enabling the children to attach huge sheets of paper to walls, fences, for drawing and painting?		
Accessibility	• are the resources, materials and equipment organized in way that is accessible to the children? For example, in vegetable racks • are they stored at the right height? • can the children see what is available, are resources labelled? • are aprons, sinks, brooms, etc., accessible to the children to allow them to take responsibility for the environment? • are drawers, cupboards and shelves easy to reach and open?		

Table 7.1 Continued

Feature	Questions	Yes/No	What do we need to improve?
Safety	• are the equipment and materials that are accessible safe for children to use? • are equipment and materials that could be dangerous if handled correctly stored and used in a way that maximizes safety? • are floorings non-slip and even?		
Aesthetics	• is the environment light? • is there a sympathetic and stimulating use of colour, form and texture in the furnishings and fittings? • does it reflect a range of cultural traditions? If home-based, do children use the wider community to explore a variety of cultural traditions? • are there spaces for the display of the children's work and that of others? • are there plants, prints and artifacts that will stimulate the children?		

Table 7.2 An environment for two- and three-dimensional development

Questions	Always? Sometimes? Never?	Changes needed?
Are the following resources available:		
• painting using a large range of brushes?		
• drawing using a range of mark-making materials and equipment?		
• textiles including materials for weaving, tapestry, knitting, batik, printing, embroidery?		
• sculpting, construction, modelling resources?		
• opportunities to investigate the properties of materials including mixing paint?		
• paper – all shapes, sizes, colour, qualities, card?		
• collage materials – bought and from the scrap bank?		
Are there opportunities for children to:		
• mix paints, glue, dough, clay?		
• choose their own material and equipment?		
• choose the most appropriate surface for the work undertaken, for example an easel, table, wall or floor?		
• combine and mix materials, for example, using large blocks as part of imaginative play?		

Table 7.2 Continued

Questions	Always? Sometimes? Never?	Change needed?
Is there space for:		
• work in progress; work to dry; storing finished work?		
• reference materials including books, prints, artifacts, examples of children's previous work, for example, portfolios?		
• displays of children's work; the work of others; artifacts to stimulate creativity? For example, at home attaching children's work to fridges and doors; by collecting images of the work of others as postcards and cut out from magazines		
• hanging mobiles and making large constructions?		
Are:		
• records of work undertaken kept in an accessible and appropriate form? For example, drawing a diagram of model; taking a photograph of a sculpture		
• places identified for children to develop their work on a particular project over time without interruptions?		
• the children aware of the use of the materials and equipment on offer?		
• the children aware of how equipment should be used and how they should behave towards each other, for example, showing respect for the work of others?		

Table 7.3 An environment for music and dance

Questions	Always? Sometimes? Never?	Changes needed?
Are the following available: • opportunities to tap, beat, scrape, blow, pluck? • a range of everyday objects for sound experimentation, such as saucepans spoons, boxes, elastic bands, flowerpots? • instruments made by children from recycled materials? • a range of instruments – string, wind, percussion, keyboard, from a variety of cultures and musical traditions? • opportunities to record sound and compose music? • opportunities to record movement and choreograph dance? • opportunities to perform music and dance? • opportunities to watch performances? • outside as well as inside?		
Is there space: • to play instruments? • to dance and move freely, for example, by moving the furniture? • to produce sound without disturbing others? • to listen to tapes and records? • to view videos of performances? • for reference books, song books, tapes, videos and records? • for drawing, and manuscript paper to record and represent dance and music?		
Are: • keyboards and scores colour coded to help children decipher and record music? • the children aware of the way in which different instruments and materials are used? • the children aware of the behaviour expected in this area, for example, care of instruments? • large and small mirrors available so that the children can observe their expressions and movement? • furnishings and fabrics used to absorb sound?		

Table 7.4 An environment for imaginative play

Questions	Always? Sometimes? Never?	Changes needed?
Are the following experiences available: • opportunities to copy and imitate? • opportunities to observe the range of roles adults undertake in the community as well as at home? • opportunities for children to take on relational, functional and character roles in their play, for example, firefighters, police, doctors, nurses, shopkeepers, super-heroes? • opportunities for children to expand the range of scenarios they use through acting out well-known stories? • opportunities for children to use structured props, unstructured props or play with no props in their play? • inside and outside play opportunities?		
Is there space for: • costumes, hats, shoes, lengths of material, jewellery, combs/brushes, ties, scarves, belts, gloves, dolls, prams, cots, wigs, baths, bottles, food, from a variety of cultures – either special collections or everyday items? • real and model kitchen equipment, cooking utensils and cleaning, from a variety of cultures? • puppets and theatre? • office equipment? • dolls and dolls' clothes from a variety of cultures?		
Are: • there more than one of each prop to aid imitative play, for example, two phones, two hats? • the children aware of the use of equipment and materials? • the children aware of how equipment should be used and how they should behave towards each other? • there enclosed areas to provide privacy?		

- Is there time for children to work alone, and/or with other children and with adults?
- Can explorations continue over time – from morning to afternoon, from day to day, over weeks – allowing children to refine and develop their ideas and representations?

The importance of peers in creative and imaginative experiences

The importance of peers cannot be overstressed, and the ways in which children are organized will determine the opportunities they have to work with a variety of children in groups of different sizes. Same- and cross-age groups have different characteristics. Working in cross-age groups enables younger children to observe and learn from more experienced learners, while the opportunity to scaffold the learning of younger children enables the older children to clarify their thinking. Children of the same age or at a comparable stage of development will often have similar interests and a desire to explore these together. The size of the group also has an impact; a pair might lead to exchanges of ideas and working together, while three or four may lead to the type of conflicts that can stimulate new connections and creativity. Experiences such as these help the children to become receptive to the ideas of others (Edwards, Gandini and Foreman 1993).

Often the hardest part for children can be the initial step towards collaborating with others. Garvey (1977), and others, have looked at children's involvement in imaginative play, the roles they adopt and the plans they use. Children can initiate imaginative play in a number of ways and signal to others the plan to be followed. They may:

- ascribe a new identity to an object, for example, by using a stick as a sword to signal the introduction of a play plan based on knights
- invest an object with animate characteristics, for example, by pretending a doll is a baby crying to indicate play based on mothers and babies
- refer to non-existent objects, for example, miming brushing teeth with a tooth brush
- adopt a role, for example, by saying 'I'm the bus driver and you're the passenger and we're going to the seaside'.

We can assist children who find it difficult to become involved to develop these skills and so help them to benefit from the full range of imaginative play. These skills are transferable and will enable the children to become involved in other creative and imaginative experiences. In imaginative play partners are often crucial. For younger children the opportunity to imitate and copy the actions of another child helps develop their play; while the elaborate narratives older children devise require a cast. Shared plans provide the narrative for imaginative play. Groups offer children an opportunity to take on different roles. The child can be:

- the star or lead
- a supporting role
- the director
- the creator and expert
- the critic
- the audience.

Again, three-dimensional representation, especially work on large constructions, can be enhanced when children can work together. The results that can be achieved by the group, the complexity of the representations produced is often far greater than those that the individual child working alone can produce. Working with other children on two-dimensional representations offers children the opportunity to see how their peers use materials and solve problems.

In music and dance what the group can produce is likely to be greater than that which the child can achieve alone. In many music and dance representations a group is essential in fully realizing the representation.

The environment we create needs to allow each child to experience a range of roles as part of groups of different sizes.

Organizing the adults to support creativity and imagination

In Chapter 6 we looked at the role of the adult and the range of roles we need to undertake. If we are to fulfil these roles we need to deploy the available adults in the most effective way. In a centre-based setting there may be a team of adults, while at home there may be only one. Whatever the number it is important that we take some time to think about the use of adult time! Adults are a valuable resource that we cannot afford to squander.

The following questions need to be addressed:

- Are adults deployed to work alongside the children as they engage in the full range of creative and imaginative experiences?
- Are adults deployed outside as well as inside?
- Do adults have time to reflect with the children, to check ideas and the progress of investigations with children?

- Is there time and space, for the adults involved with the children, to meet to discuss, record, assess, plan and develop their practice and reach a shared understanding?
- Is there time for adults to record and document the children's representations?
- If in a centre-based setting, are the children's family and friends fully involved?
- Do the children use the adults as a resource?
- Is there time for adults to take on a range of roles:
  - observing the children
  - guiding, suggesting and explaining
  - re-starting when they have become confused or lost
  - helping the children overcome difficulties and become re-motivated
  - taking children by the hand and showing them how to do something?

Conclusion

Young children and the adults responsible for them find themselves in a wide variety of settings. They may occupy purpose-built premises, share premises with others, and/or be at home. Each setting will have its own frustrations and limitations as well as its own particular ambience. All can be used to promote young children's creativity and imagination if we, the adults involved, use our own creativity and imagination.

Summary

This chapter has established:

- the importance of creating the right emotional environment
- the importance of creating the right physical environment
- ensuring that there is sufficient space to be creative and imaginative
- ensuring that there is sufficient time for creative and imaginative explorations
- that working with adults and other children is important and needs careful organization.

Further reading

Edwards, C., Gandini, L. and Forman, G. (eds) (1993) *The Hundred Languages of Children*. New York: Ablex Press.
  This book describes the Reggio Emilia approach to early childhood education.
Garvey, C. (1977) *Play*. London: Fontana.
  Chapter 6 looks at pretend and imaginative play.
Goldschmied, E. and Jackson, S. (1994) *People Under Three: Young Children in Day Care*. London: Routledge.
  Chapter 2 looks at organizing space for living, learning and playing.

Things to think about

- How does the layout of your setting promote creativity?

- What are the limitations?

- What action can you take?

- How does your organization of time promote creativity and imagination?

- What are the limitations?

- What action can you take?

- How do you organize the children to promote opportunities for creativity and imagination?

- What else can you do?

- How do you deploy the available adults and resources?

- Can they be used more effectively?

8

Extending children's experiences

Introduction

This chapter will look at:

- why it is important to extend children's access to creative and imaginative experiences
- using the local environment
- using practising artists, musicians, performers and crafts people
- using galleries, museums and live performances
- using displays
- appraising and appreciating the work of others.

Why it is important to extend children's access to creative and imaginative experiences

Creativity and imagination need stimulation. Exploring the local environment and sharing the creative and imaginative representations of adults in the community inducts children into their own culture, while exposure to the representations of other communities introduces them to cultures other than their own. If children are to be creative and imaginative we must feed and inspire them by widening their experiences.

When we are planning opportunities which extend the range of creative and imaginative experiences usually on offer, we need to:

- decide what we want from the experience, for example, how will it build on children's previous learning and development, create new opportunities for representation and creativity, provide a stimulus for future learning and development?
- decide how much time is available and how can it best be used. Be realistic about how much can be accomplished in the time available.
- prepare ourselves and the children well. Talk to the children beforehand to explain the purpose of the experience and what they will be doing, but leave some element of surprise.
- ensure that there are sufficient adults for the number of children involved. If we are leaving the immediate premises, what is the adult to child ratio for the setting? Discuss the purpose, aims and expectations with helpers beforehand.
- think about how the children will represent their experiences. If they are going to draw, is there a board to lean on and a way of attaching the paper? If they are going to record sounds to inspire music, can the tape recorder record with sufficient clarity? If cameras are used, is there a tripod or something similar for the children to rest it on?
- if we are going somewhere new, how do we get there? A visit before we take the children is a good idea. We can use this visit to gather relevant information, for example, what particular aspects of the location will most interest the children, does the journey involve potential problems (such as long escalators) and where are the toilets!
- think about how the children will share their experience with others and how they will build on it during the following days, for instance, through role play.

Using the local environment

The local environment is part of the children's everyday experience. By using this environment to promote their creativity and imagination we are:

- encouraging children to value and take pride in their neighbourhood
- increasing their understanding of the community they come from
- sharpening their awareness of the world around them
- helping them to look in detail at the familiar and see new possibilities
- developing their visual literacy
- building on their previous learning.

We can make use of:

- *the changing seasons* by observing and recording the changes in the natural and manufactured world
- *community festivals* by drawing on the cultural, religious and social traditions of the district
- *buildings* by investigating homes, places of work and worship, bus and train stations, local landmarks.

At first sight some local environments may appear to offer little opportunity to develop creativity and imagination. For example, a run-down inner city area may lack well-kept parks, listed buildings and carefully designed public spaces. But closer examination may reveal a wealth of opportunities. The old Victorian houses have intricate mouldings and stained glass, and the trees that line the streets reflect the changing seasons. Dandelions grow on the derelict building plots. Community festivals bring displays of light, colour, music and dance on to the streets. All these add richness to the children's lives and can inspire a range of representations.

Guidelines:

1 Think about the various aspects of the local environment and the possibilities for creativity and imagination they could provide.
2 You may be using a garden, school grounds or going further afield. Make sure there is plenty of time for the children to observe, discuss and record whatever aspect of the local environment they are focusing on.
3 If you are visiting places of work, such as shops or fire stations, make sure you have spoken to those who work there before you arrive and that they agree to your visit.
4 Make links with people in the local community who can alert you to events, such as fairs, carnivals, etc., so that the children can be involved in the preparation as well as the final event.
5 Think about the equipment children will need, for example, magnifying glasses to look at plants and surfaces in detail.
6 Do not overlook the potential of the familiar. Looking at the building they are in, with a creative and imaginative perspective, can open children's eyes. They can identify the different materials used and decide why a particular material is used for a particular purpose. They can look for the elements of art – patterns, shapes, colour, tone, form and see how they are used individually and together. They can assess the aesthetic qualities of the building – how does it make them feel, which areas do they like best and why, how would they change things?

Example

As part of her evidence of competence in National Vocational Qualifications for Child Care and Education, Rosie submitted, in her portfolio, a record of the work she and a group of 3-year-olds had undertaken in their local environment. Rosie had observed the children's interest in the local flora during a journey to the library and after discussion with the children they decided to investigate this aspect of their environment more fully. The children and Rosie spent an afternoon walking around the area looking for as many different plants as possible. They found a variety of flowers (dandelions, docks, thistles, daisies, viola, cow parsley), grasses and leafy plants growing wild on the canal verge, between paving stones and on the edge of derelict sites. Using reference books they discovered the name of each specimen. They recorded their observations with drawings, rubbings and photographs, and Rosie wrote down comments the children made as they explored. On their return, they created a display to share with other children and their parents.

Using practising artists, musicians, performers and crafts people

Another way to extend children's experiences is to bring artists and crafts people into the setting. They may be used to:

- put on a performance or display
- demonstrate their work to the children
- work alongside or with the children.

Such experiences offer children the chance to see the visual and performing arts in action. Through these experiences children become aware of the role and function of creativity and imagination in society and gain insights into their own and other cultures.

Working alongside artists gives children an opportunity to find out what is involved in their work. They can find out:

- what and how equipment and materials are used
- how equipment is cared for, for example, the care of paints and brushes
- the whole process involved, for instance, from preparation, execution of performance to clearing away and packing up
- the problems and practicalities, for example, transporting musical instrument and large pieces of work
- the importance of having an audience for your work.

Guidelines:

1 What is the aim and focus of the experience? How are you going to use the artist's or crafts person's time with the children? How will you follow up the project? How will you fund it? What can you afford to spend?
2 Choose your artist with care. Some excellent crafts people and artists are not good teachers! If possible use the recommendation of a colleague, parent or friend. You will also wish to make sure that the person you use is a suitable person to work with young children by taking up references.
3 Be creative and imaginative. Parents and friends often have skills they can share or local arts forums and regional arts councils may be able to recommend someone.
4 Draw up a clear list of your expectations to share with artist or performer beforehand.
5 Meet with the artist or performer beforehand to discuss your expectations of the projects; the time and length of each session; the needs and abilities of the children; the number of children they will work with; practical arrangements including storage of equipment and materials.
6 Prepare yourself and the children well. Talk to the children beforehand, introduce them to the work of the artist or the field of performing or visual art they are going to explore.
7 Identify a suitable project space where the artists and children can work and materials and equipment be stored.
8 Record the progress of the project and the children's response. This will enable the children to reflect on the experience and share it with others.
9 Celebrate the end of the project with a display or performance.
10 Be prepared for some disruption and changes to the usual pattern of the day.

Visits to galleries, museums, theatres and other venues for the visual and performing arts

Visits to galleries and museums offer children the opportunity to examine real works of art at close range. The experience of seeing a sculpture or a painting life size, and the opportunity to examine the texture of the surface, is very different from looking at a print or model. Children are often drawn to paintings with a strong narrative element. During a recent trip to

---

Example

As part of a focus on 'Celebrations' a group of 2-, 3- and 4-year-olds became aware of banners and their use in festivals, parties and other celebrations. In response the centre staff arranged for the children to work with Cathy, a local artist who makes banners. The purpose of the project was to introduce the children to banner-making and the print process. The project started with a workshop for staff. This introduced the staff to the banner-making process and print-making techniques. They produced a small banner to share with the children and demonstrate the techniques they would be using. Cathy then came and worked with groups of children on two banners. They:

- produced their own images to go on the banners
- used a variety of techniques including finger painting and silk screen printing to transfer their images onto the banner.

Cathy then pressed and prepared the banner for hanging. The children had an opportunity to develop their understanding of printing. They learnt how images could be transferred to the banner (see Figure 8.1), they discovered that images could be repeated and reversed, they found out more about how colours mix and merge. They realized the importance of having a space to work undisturbed and the need to continue work on the banner over a number of days. At the end of the project the children shared their work with their parents and others in the centre through a display of the banners and the process involved.

---

the Tate Gallery a group of nursery children revealed that their favourite painting was 'Ophelia'. They were interested in why she was lying in the water and wanted to know what her mother would say when she went home with a wet dress. But they were also fascinated by the abstract paintings hanging in nearby galleries and commented on the artists' use of colour and the texture of paint.

The experience of being part of an audience is a powerful one. Excitement and atmosphere build as the audience wait for the performance to start. For the period of the performance the everyday world is in suspense and the world of the imagination takes over. The aspects of the experience that engage the children may surprise the adult. For example, one child spent an entire performance watching the way in which the lights changed, fascinated by the different effects that could be created.

Figure 8.1   Simon, aged 3 years 8 months, working with Cathy to produce a banner.

Guidelines:

1 Many galleries, theatres and dance companies have education officers. Contact them and ask their advice. If possible, arrange for them to accompany your visit.
2 Bear in mind the age of the children, what will appeal to them?
3 Do not try to pack too much in on a visit to a gallery. It is better to look at one painting in detail than to try to cover the whole gallery.
4 Find out if it is acceptable to take photographs to record the children's experience before you visit.
5 Talk to the children beforehand about galleries and theatres. For example, what do they look like, how do people behave in them, what do you do inside them? Talk about what they will be doing and seeing. Look at pictures, videos and books.
6 Bring the supplies necessary for the age group you are taking. For example, spare underwear or nappies for inevitable accidents and a first-aid kit.

Using displays

Displays can be large or small. They may consist of an arrangement of interesting objects and materials on a window sill or be spread along a large corridor. Whatever their size, displays offer children the opportunity to:

- celebrate and share their own work, in process as well as finished
- observe and handle the work of other people across cultures and times
- see how others have handled materials and solved problems
- develop their aesthetic awareness and visual literacy
- stimulate and extend their range of representations
- explore and focus on particular aspects of representation, for example:
  - use of colour, texture, line
  - particular sorts of artifacts – clothes, shoes, costumes
  - different representations – printing, drawing, textiles.

Guidelines:

1 Think about who the display is aimed at. Is it accessible to them? Is it as near as possible to the eye level of the intended viewer? (Figure 8.2).
2 What is its aim? For example, celebrating children's representations, improving the aesthetic qualities of the environment, sharing children's achievement?
3 How are children involved? For example, did they help to choose the items and arrange them; will they dictate the captions to be used?
4 Are names, labels and explanations legible? Are there examples of handwritten as well as printed captions? Is the title clear, the wording grammatically correct with correct spelling and punctuation? Are appropriate scripts used that reflect the languages used by the children?
5 Does the background contrast and enhance the display or detract from it? Are different backgrounds used for different effects, for example, paper, corrugated card or material?
6 Are drawings, prints and paintings mounted?
7 Are mobiles and suspended work also used?
8 Is the display well laid out?
9 Are three-dimensional representations displayed? Are blocks or boxes used to vary the height of the display?

Appraising and appreciating the work of others

Opportunities to explore the work of others helps children to develop their critical skills and to bring these skills to their own work. By looking at and

Figure 8.2   A display of sunflowers from a variety of times and cultures

listening to the work of others, children are able to enhance their own work. Seeing or hearing how other people have tackled problems offers starting points to tackle their own challenges.

The constructive feedback of other adults and children in response to their own work is helpful to children and assists them in refining their representations.

In order to share and discuss their views the children need to have access to an appropriate vocabulary. The vocabulary they use should help them:

- to describe
- to evaluate
- to explain their own intentions and what they perceive to be the intentions of others.

It is important to ensure that:

- children are encouraged to use their own words to describe what they see, hear, touch and feel

- new and specialist vocabulary is introduced in a meaningful context
- children are encouraged to use an accurate vocabulary
- they are introduced to the elements of music, dance and art to describe what they perceive
- they look at the process involved as well as the end-product.

Think in advance of the comments and questions you can use to stimulate discussion. How you will follow up and use the observations the children made.

However, it is important to remember that art, dance and music are languages in their own right and many of their qualities are not captured by words. Media, such as music, are able to reach us in a very direct way that is beyond words, they have the ability to transcend words. We can say things with music that we could never say with words.

Conclusion

By giving the children rich, first-hand experiences of the visual and performing arts, and the local environment, we feed their imagination and creativity. There are practical difficulties in arranging visits – transport, accessibility, sufficient number of adults – and sometimes we can find ourselves wondering if it is all worth it. But the enrichment that such experiences bring to young children's lives and the quality of creative and imaginative representations that result, mean that we must use our ingenuity and imagination to ensure that all children have these opportunities.

Summary

This chapter has established that:

- children need opportunities to explore their local environment
- children benefit from exposure to the work of others and opportunities to work with artist and crafts people
- displays have an important role to play in developing children's visual and aesthetic awareness
- appraising and appreciating the work of others helps children to develop their own work.

Further reading

Manser, S. (1995) *Artists in Residence: A Teacher's Handbook*. London: London Arts Board.
This handbook gives guidance to those wanting to work with artists in school. It looks at the benefits to be gained and the types of work that can be undertaken.

Things to think about

- How do you use the local environment to encourage creativity and imagination?

- Have you made contact with artists, crafts people, musicians and performers who can share their work with the children?

- How often do the children for whom you are responsible have the opportunity to visit museums and galleries?

- How do you use displays?

9

Planning, implementing, observing, recording and assessing

Introduction

This chapter will examine:

- the importance of the planning, implementing, observing, recording and assessing cycle

- the importance of involving children

- the importance of involving parents

- the cycle in practice.

The importance of the planning, implementing, observing, recording and assessing cycle

In the previous chapters I have outlined why creativity and imagination are important, the range of experiences children should have access to; how children's development influences their access to and use of creative and imaginative experiences; the creative process; the role of the adult and organization of the environment. This chapter will look at how we ensure that we incorporate all these elements into our practice as part of a continuous cycle. Planning and implementing, observing, recording and assessing are the stages in this cycle.

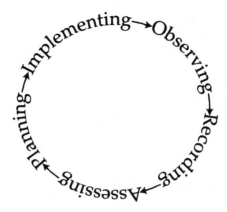

In our work with children we need to ensure that each stage of the cycle is in place and in use. The cycle helps us to think through how we will:

- ensure that the experience we offer matches the particular needs and interest of individuals and groups – why are we offering this experience at this time?
- organize children's access to creative and imaginative opportunities – is it better for children to work alone or as part of a group?
- organize our own role – will we be observing, facilitating, demonstrating, acting as critical friend?
- record and assess the children's responses – how has the experience promoted the children's creativity and imagination?
- use the information we gather to inform the next cycle – what should we do next?

We are looking for teachable moments, chances to put our goals for the children's learning into practice by making use of every opportunity.

Sometimes we progress through the stages of the cycle in the space of minutes, maybe in response to a spontaneous event. On other occasions, the cycle spreads over months or years. For example, we watch children over time to see how they are responding to the creative and imaginative environment we have created, we analyse our observations and plan our modifications.

The cycle is also used to support children's learning and development over the medium term and we will be looking at examples of this later in the chapter.

Whether the cycle is short, medium or long term, it needs to be manageable, clear and involve all those who have the children's interest at heart. These include:

- the adults who are responsible for the children

Example

Leon, who is 5 years old, and Ann, who is 3, were sitting at the table with an adult, eating lunch. They heard the roadworks going on outside. 'Chi, boom, chi, boom, chi, boom that's the sound' said Ann in a deep voice. 'The drill is going bizz, bizz, bizz' adds Leon, using a higher pitch. The adult responded by joining in and changing the pitch, making each of the sounds that the children had identified get higher and lower. Ann commented 'That's like the organ downstairs, it goes up and down.' The adult suggested using the organ later to make the sounds of the roadworks and the children agreed with enthusiasm. During the afternoon the children used the organ and were introduced to the terms high and low to describe the musical elements they have identified.

- the children themselves
- the parents, if children are attending settings in the absence of their parents.

The importance of involving children

Creative and imaginative representations are about the individual, their personal response to the world and the ways in which they choose to represent this. Children's intentions are not captured by most adult definitions of the visual and performing arts (Matthews 1994). For this reason it is essential to involve children in the assessment and planning of their work. We need to find out from children:

- What were their intentions?
- Why have they used materials or ideas in that particular way?
- Does the result satisfy them, are they happy with it?
- What would they like to do or know next?

Obviously children's ability to engage in conversations of this sort increases with age. But with the support of a well-known and receptive adult they can start to take part in this process from a young age. In the early stages adults will be using behavioural clues to gain an insight into the children's views. For example, are they concentrating intently on the experience? Do they show satisfaction on completion? Do they return to the activity? Later we can use verbal clues. For example, has the child given a label to the representation? Is the child responsive to our commentary on the representation? Once children have developed the vocabulary to describe their own representations the presence of a receptive adult who listens to their explanations, asks questions and makes comments that demonstrate genuine interest is crucial. Our comments are most useful when they help children to recognize the elements of art, music and dance they have used in their representation and make links between their use of these elements and the use that others have made of them. A trusting relationship, honesty and a shared understanding with an adult provides the security children need to discuss their representations, reflect on their learning and identify the next step.

The importance of involving parents

Children's homes and family life often provide the ideas and themes that are reflected in their creative and imaginative representations. For this reason alone, adults who work with children other than their own need to involve parents in their assessment and planning of children's experiences. Without the input of parents we will lack access to these major influences on children's representations and our assessments will be partial. Parents have a right to be involved in all aspects of their children's learning. The role of nursery staff, childminders, teachers and others is to find ways of ensuring that this right is evident in their practice.

Each setting needs to identify the best way to involve the parents of children in their particular group. Some parents may be concerned about

---

Example

Mona, aged 6, described and evaluated her drawing (see Figure 9.1). 'It's about a little girl who, once upon a time, wanted to go on a big girl's swing and her mummy said, "No! little girls go on little girls swings", and the little girl was sad and waited to become a big girl [*teacher asks how she made the girl look sad*]. She's sitting by herself not playing with her friends. I used crayons because they're easier than paint [*teacher asks why*]. They don't drip and you can make the colours stay in the right place [*teacher asks how she chose the colours*]. Red is my favourite colour [*referring to colour of little girl's dress*]. I used blue for the sky because it's blue and green for the grass because it's green. [*teacher asks "Does the picture look the way you wanted it to look?"*]. I did the swing right, not the bit at the top that shouldn't be there [*refers to extra line on the frame of the swing*]. The little girl looks sweet! ahh! I'm good at drawing apple trees. I'm good at drawing.'

Figure 9.1 A sad little girl and a swing.

gender issues, for example, that their son enjoys dressing up as part of imaginative play. Other parents, especially as children get older, may be concerned that time spent on creative and imaginative experiences would be better used for other purposes, for example, literacy and numeracy. We need to take concerns of this nature seriously and take the time and effort

---

Example

Mark's parents discuss their son's art portfolio with his teacher. Mark is 5 years old and in the reception class. 'He really likes drawing. At home he has loads of pens and felt-tips and he uses them whenever he wants. Sometimes we sit with him while he draws but most of the time he gets on with it himself. He asks when he gets stuck though. When he was trying to draw our house [see Figure 9.2] he wanted to know how to draw the people in bed sideways. So we showed him. Of course he watches his older sister. She shows him how to do things and then a few days later you see what she's taught him in one of his drawings. At one time we were worried that all he did was drawing, painting, sticking . . . he wasn't interested in anything else. But now he's really good at writing, he can write his own name neatly, much better than some of the other children.'

Figure 9.2   Our house.

to explain the value of creativity and imagination and the contribution they make to other areas of the curriculum. If parents feel confident that we are clear about what we are doing with their children and why we are doing it they will be reassured. We can involve parents in assessing and planning children's creative and imaginative experiences by:

- ensuring a welcoming atmosphere
- organizing occasions for staff and parents to meet to discuss individual children's work, such as regular meetings to look at samples of children's work, discuss observations and draw up plans to support the children over the next few months
- creating opportunities to discuss creativity and imagination and their value to children, for example, through curriculum workshops and displays of children's work.

The cycle in practice

Our aim is to extend children's learning by identifying children's current level of understanding, and planning activities, experiences and explorations that will lead them to the next stage. To do this we draw on:

- our knowledge of the attitudes, skills and knowledge associated with different elements of the creative and imaginative framework, which we looked at in Chapter 3
- our knowledge of the likely patterns of development, which we looked at in Chapter 4
- our knowledge of the creative process, which we looked at in Chapter 5
- Vygotsky's theory of the zone of proximal development and Bruner's concept of scaffolding, which we looked at in Chapter 6
- the environment we have prepared, which we looked at in Chapter 7.

In some settings plans and assessments will be made with reference to:

- Desirable Outcomes for Children's Learning
- Art in the National Curriculum
- Music in the National Curriculum
- Physical Education in the National Curriculum which contains Dance.

We can plan and evaluate creative and imaginative experiences in a number of ways:

- through the use of themes and cross-curricular approaches
- through using children's current schema
- by responding to children's spontaneous interest
- through specific activities and experiences that focus on creativity and imagination.

While, in reality, the different stages of the cycle overlap and spill into each other it is helpful to look at the role of each stage.

Planning

This is the stage in the cycle when we think about the experience we are to offer:

- How is it based on our observations of the children's needs and interests?
- How does it relate to previous experiences?
- What experiences will be included?
- What are the possibilities for learning?
- Which aspects of Desirable Outcomes or National Curriculum do we hope to address?
- How will we introduce the experience to the children?
- How will we organize, materials, ourselves and the children?
- What role or roles will we be undertaking?

- How will the children be involved in planning the development of the experience?
- How will parents be involved?

Implementing

This is the stage in the cycle when we engage with the children in whatever role is most appropriate. This involves:

- introducing the experience and purpose clearly to the children
- helping them to make the link with their previous learning
- introducing new skills or concepts
- ensuring that the children have the opportunity to influence the progress of the experience
- scaffolding their learning as necessary
- acting as facilitator if required
- responding to the comments and observations they make (see Figure 9.3)
- giving them the opportunity to explore and play with the ideas or concepts introduced
- leaving time for new connections to be made and creativity to take place.

Observing

While we engage with the children we observe their uptake and response to what is on offer.

- How are they using the equipment and materials that are available? (see Figure 9.4)
- What elements of art, music or dance are they using and how?
- What skills and attitudes are they demonstrating and which do they need to develop?
- What are the children's comments and how do they demonstrate their knowledge and understanding?
- What is their actual level of development?

Observations may be written down and included as part of the children's records. Whether written or not they should be used to assess the children and plan the next steps in their learning.

Figure 9.3 A key worker and group of 3- and 4-year-olds discussing the differences and similarities in skin tones before creating self-portraits.

Figure 9.4 A key worker observing a 2-year-old painting and offering support by his obvious pleasure in her representation.

Recording

We need to find manageable ways of recording our observations. It is not possible to record every aspect of children's creative and imaginative experiences. If we attempted to do so we would spend all our time in the role of observer! We need to record that which is significant, which is going to help to assess and plan for the children. Our focus should be on recording children's significant progress or difficulties. Over time, these records will provide evidence of the children's learning and development. We can record children's creative and imaginative development in a variety of ways. These may include:

1 *Written observations of the children and transcripts of their comments*: These are particularly useful for aspects of creativity and imaginative experiences which have no product, such as imaginative play.
2 *Portfolios of the children's representations*: These can include actual work products such as drawings, paintings or collage (large paintings or those containing layers of thick paint are better included as photographs); photographs of three-dimensional constructions; textiles and imaginative play
3 *Recording*: Video and audio tapes can be used to record dance and music
4 *Assessments and reviews of progress*: Access to their records helps children to reflect on their past learning and thinking about the next steps.

Assessing and evaluating

This is the stage in the cycle when we evaluate the children's experience. This may be in the form of a work product, observations of the the process they went through, or a transcript of their comments. Children's representations can be analysed and assessed in a number of ways. Sometimes their drawings are used to assess their emotional state and general intellectual ability. This may involve giving children's work meanings that the children themselves did not intend (Matthews 1994 and Cox 1992). When we assess and evaluate their work we should concentrate on:

- What have the children achieved and how does it match with the aims we identified at the planning stage?
- What is the children's assessment of the experience? What do they think they have achieved?
- What creative and imaginative knowledge attitudes and skills have the children shown in their use of materials and equipment that they have not demonstrated before?

- Which elements of art, music and dance have they used and to what effect?
- How have the children worked as part of a group or individually?
- How has their use of materials or ideas demonstrated creativity and imagination?
- What new connections have they made?
- What is their understanding of the actual level of development and how do we help them to progress to the next stage?
- What have we achieved? How did our plans work in practice?

Planning the next steps

This is the return to the start of the cycle. Having planned, implemented and assessed we decide how we will use the information we now have to inform our planning of the next cycle.

Example – Exploring sunflowers with a group of 2- and 3-year-olds

Planning

The children had grown sunflowers in the garden and staff used their continued interest to:

- introduce them to representations from their own and other cultures and times
- extend the range and quality of their representations.

They planned to do this by:

- helping the children to create a sunflower display
- using the display to show children how other people have represented sunflowers
- supporting the children in using this information as they wished in their own representations.

They prepared by:

- gathering representations of sunflowers for the children to use, for example, a wooden sculpture from Bali, a print of Van Gogh's 'Sunflowers', images on wrapping paper and margarine boxes
- ensuring that there was a wide range of resources for the children to use
- identifying possibilities for learning – the knowledge, skills and attitudes.

Implementation

- staff introduced the exploration to the children by linking it to their interest in the sunflowers they had grown
- they showed the children the sunflower representations they had collected and invited them to bring their own examples from home, for example, one child brought in a hat patterned with sunflowers
- they invited the children to compare the real sunflowers with the representations of sunflowers and discussed similarities and differences, which ones children liked best, the materials and techniques that had been used
- they drew children's attention to the range of resources available
- children made their own representations of the sunflowers, selecting from the wide range of materials available, for example, using blocks, collage materials, water colours, poster paints, printing
- the children worked alone, in pairs or as part of a group (see Figure 9.5)
- the different resources available enabled children to focus on the aspects of the sunflowers that interested them.

Observation, recording and assessment

The staff observed the children as they worked and recorded the children's comments. Below is a sample from one child's record as it relates to the exploration of sunflowers. (This sample is only part of the record kept by the key worker.)

Observation sheet for Julie, aged 4 years 2 months, at time of first observation

---

Please comment on the child's creative and imaginative development (see centre policy for guidance)

Date	Observation	Support to further development
7/7	J looking at sunflowers in nursery garden, related them to sunflowers grown at home. Able to describe colour ('it' sunshine yellow'), shape/form ('there's a bit in the middle, with petals around the outside') and size ('it's smaller than mine at home') discussion continued in key worker group	organize visit, key group visit to J's home to compare nursery sunflower with home sunflower

8/7 discussion on walk to home – connected shape/form of sunflower to sun design on garden gate (photo + comments in portfolio) associated yellow on school sign with sunflowers (photo + comments in portfolio)	help J to make display of photos and comments with rest of group
11/7 J + Amy used blocks to create sunflower based on core and radial design of gate. At my suggestion recorded design by drawing plan on large sheet of paper attached to wall to put in their portfolios	J appears to be interested in representing sunflowers using core and radial design. Extend by introducing new materials
14/7 representing sunflowers using (1) match-sticks (2) pre-cut tissue circles – large circles in middle, smaller circles around edges. Items placed with accuracy, preoccupied with distance between each petal being the the same (see portfolio)	create display of sunflower representations with J and other children to extend their under-standing of images
18/7 observed examining items on display, brought in wrapping paper from home, asked about illustration of sunflowers using watercolour and wet paper ('how did he do that – sunflowers in the rain?') put sunflower cushion over face said 'I'm a sunflower'	(1) explore representing sunflowers using movement and gesture (2) introduce watercolour + wet paper
22/7 compared effect of wet and dry paper, liked wet paper best ('it's gone fuzzy'). Mixing colours – interested in matching shades used to those seen on petals ('it's gone green not orange – that's not right') realized that colour changed if more water used. I introduced the idea that the colour was more intense if less water used	more work on mixing secondary colours from primary colours and how to lighten and darken hues
23/7 J, Amy and Emma used movement to represent sunflowers – rotating ('this sunflower is twirling . . .') curling and stretching ('this is me growing	find out if children want to (1) develop sunflower movements into dance (2) develop

up . . .') swaying ('the sunflower in the wind . . .') used bells ('this is the sunflower singing')	piece of music based on sunflowers
25/7 J commented on samples of her work and chose selection for portfolio featuring her work on sunflowers	discuss with parents and plan next steps

Figure 9.5 Two children worked together to produce a life-size representation of a sunflower.

Next steps

As the exploration progressed the children became interested in matching the colours they saw to the colours they mixed. The staff noted that the children lacked the vocabulary to describe these shades. Next steps:

- use the children's previous experience of mixing primary colours to produce secondary colours to introduce them to the idea of shades
- ensure access to a range of materials and resources including water colour brushes, paints in block and powder form and food colouring, white plastic bowls for mixing, sheets of white paper of different weights and textures
- deploy adult to work alongside the children to help them comment on the process involved
- encourage the children to describe the colours they create.

Example – Exploring drums with a group of 3- and 4-year-olds

Planning

The aim was to build on the children's self-initiated explorations of the drums and use this to extend their understanding of the instrument. The adults prepared by:

- collecting a range of drums for the children to experiment with
- collecting books for reference
- arranging for a drummer to visit later in the day
- identifying the possibilities for learning – knowledge of the range of drums (tabla, snare, bongos, African drums), understanding that the way in which a drum is hit alters the sound produced, knowledge of the sounds that can be produced and introducing musical elements to describe the sounds heard such as high/low, loud/quiet, working as part of group, offering help to others and taking turns.

Implementation

- the adult introduced the exploration by linking it to the children's self- initiated exploration of drums
- the adult explained about the planned visit from a drummer
- she discussed with the children – had they seen drums being played? How did they think drums produced sounds? How many different sounds did they think drums made? How do you play drums?
- the children used the collection of drums and reference books available in the room to: identify the different types of drums, examine and identify the different parts of the drums, to produce different sounds using, hands, fingers and beaters and described the sounds they had made
- some of the children used the pencils and paper available to record the different parts of the drum
- the children decide to combine the drums to make a drum kit ready for the visiting drummer. With help from the adult and information

from the reference books they identified the different elements that make up a drum kit. They discussed which of the drums available looked most like those in the books and arranged them as shown (see Figure 9.6).

Observation, recording and assessing

The adult recorded the children's observations and comments, for example, Dave knew that drummers played drums and said he had seen this on television. By the end of the session he was able to describe:

- the difference between drums and other instruments ('you bang drums . . . with your hand or a stick')
- the range of sounds that can be produced ('if you use your fingers it sounds like rain . . . the soft beater is quieter than the stick')
- the different parts of the drum ('that's the shell . . . that's the skin . . . you hit the skin to make the sound')
- the difference between the snare and tabla drum ('that's made from wood, that's from metal . . . the tabla is taller and its shiny . . . its got strings on it . . . you use your hands').

Dave was able to use his hands and beaters to make loud and quiet sounds and use the correct terms. He chose to draw the tabla drum from the display of drums.

Figure 9.6 Dave and Linda, aged 3, created their own drum kit.

Next steps

- visit from drummer to enable the children to practise their skills on wider selection of drums
- making their own drum
- recording the sounds of drums using their own symbols.

Example – Developing imaginative play with a group of 1- and 2-year-olds

Planning

On their way to the local park the attention of a group of 1- and 2-year-olds was taken by roadworks that were in progress. The adults stopped to let the children have a closer look. They helped the children to identify the different vehicles involved, the traffic lights that were directing the traffic and the clothes the workmen were wearing. They introduced the children to new vocabulary, such as bulldozer and tar. The children were excited by the experience and the adults decided to build on this interest. They:

- gathered together a range of small toys such as trucks and play people
- cleared a large space in the room so that the children could play freely
- emptied sand on to the floor for the children to use in their play
- thought about the learning possibilities the play might offer, for example, the opportunity to represent their experiences, introduction to using narrative in their play, an increase in their vocabulary to include words related to the experience.

Implementation

The next morning the children found the play materials waiting for them.

- the adults reminded the children of their experience of roadworks the previous day
- the adults also played with the materials alongside the children, making up brief narratives, for example, re-telling the children's visit to the roadworks
- the children quickly joined in. Initially, they concentrated on moving the toys with appropriate sound effects but gradually they started to relate what they were doing to the other children in the group, for instance, introducing simple sequences where they each took play people to the pretend park and took turns on the slide

- some of the children began to introduce more complex narratives involving an accident when a motor-cyclist went through a red light!
- the adults supported their play by discreetly providing resources as the children needed them, helping the children to negotiate potential conflicts and offering suggestions for new episodes in the story.

Observing, recording and assessing

At the end of the day the adults discussed the children's use of materials and recorded their observations about the success of the experience as a whole. They also recorded the significant progress that individual children had made. They concluded:

- the children had responded positively to the experience, all the children in the group had been involved
- with support, they had been able to play together as a group and joined together to produce new narratives
- individual children had been able to represent the aspects of the experience that most appealed to them, for example, Kevin had remembered seeing a rubbish truck trying to negotiate its way through the roadworks and it was this aspect that he represented. He developed his narrative to include an imagined episode involving the rubbish truck taking away the wrong things!
- the adults found that the children were responding to the new vocabulary they were introducing and using it for themselves
- the children were able to describe what they had done.

Next steps

- to return to the site to allow the children to compare their representation with the real roadworks
- to take a picture of the site for future use
- to extend the range of small props available to allow the children to extend their storylines
- to record the children's narrative and use them with the photographs to make a book as a permanent record of the experience.

Conclusion

The examples given in this chapter (and in the rest of the book) are drawn from real life. They are not meant to be perfect models. Their purpose is to show how real groups of adults are trying to provide for young children's creative and imaginative development with all the restraints and pressures that are part of everyday life.

The planning, implementing, observing, recording and assessing cycle

Conclusion

In this book I have tried to stress the importance of creativity and imagination for young children and the society of which they are part. Promoting creativity is not about giving children access to expensive equipment and materials, or providing exotic experiences, but it is to do with how we maximize our use of the environment we find ourselves in and draw out the most from our interactions with the children. Nor is it about trying to accelerate children's learning and development by intensive cramming. Our aim is to deepen their understanding and encourage a lifelong appreciation of, and involvement in, creativity and imagination.

Let us return to the example that I used in the introduction. James and Daniel are engaged in what Vygotsky describes as the highest level of thought in early childhood. They have created their own reality and can sustain this through the power of their imagination. This ability will enable them to solve problems, reach new understandings and perceive abstract meanings. It will enable them to become the creative, imaginative, and compassionate people we need them to be.

is not an end in itself but a means to an end. The purpose of the cycle is to ensure that all children have access to the creative and imaginative opportunities we believe they need so that they can become the most creative and imaginative individuals they can be.

Summary

This chapter has:

- identified the stages in the planning, implementing, observing, recording and assessing cycle as they relate to the development of creativity and imagination
- shown how these stages follow on and overlap
- offered real-life examples of this process in practice.

Further reading

Cox, C. (1992) *Children's Drawings*. London: Penguin.
Chapter 5 looks at the diagnostic use of children's drawings.
Matthews, J. (1994) *Helping Young Children to Draw and Paint in Early Childhood*. London: Hodder and Stoughton.
Chapter 9 looks at how adults can help children to draw and paint, and the importance of record-keeping.
Westminster City Council (1996) *Great Expectations: A Curriculum for the Under Fives*. Westminster: Education and Leisure Department.
Sections 5, 6 and 7 offer a systematic approach to planning, recording, assessing and evaluating provision for young children.

Things to think about

- How do you plan children's creative and imaginative experiences?

- How do you ensure that these plans are implemented?

- How do you assess children's creative and imaginative development?

- How do you assess your own practice?

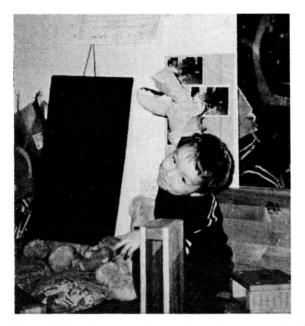

Figure C1.1 Stuart, aged 2 years 3 months, engaged in the highest level of thought in early childhood while using puppets to act out a narrative.

Bibliography

Athey, C. (1990) *Extending Thought in Young Children: A Parent–Teacher Partnership*. London: Paul Chapman.

Bettelheim, B. (1976) *The Uses of Enchantment: The Meaning and Importance of Fairy Tales*. London: Thames and Hudson.

Bloom, B. S. and Sosniak, L. A. (1981) Talent development vs schooling. *Educational Leadership*, 27: 86–94.

Bruce, T. (1987) *Early Childhood Education*. London: Hodder and Stoughton.

Bruner, J. (1975) The ontogenesis of speech acts. *Journal of Child Language*, 2: 1–9.

Bruner, J. (1977) *The Process of Education*. Cambridge, Mass.: Harvard University Press.

Bruner, J. (1982) 'What is representation?', in M. Roberts and J. Tamburrini (eds) *Child Development 0–5*. Edinburgh: Holmes McDougall.

Bruner, J. (1986) *Actual Minds, Possible Worlds*. Harvard: Harvard University Press.

Calouste Gulbenkian (1982) *The Arts in School*. London: Calouste Gulbenkian Foundation.

Cecil, L. M., Gray, M. M., Thornburg, K. R. and Ispa, J. (1985) Curiosity-exploration-play: the early childhood mosaic. *Early Child Development and Care*, 19: 199–217.

Chukovsky, K. (1963) *From Two to Five*. Berkeley, CA.: University of California Press.

Claxton, G. (1984) *Live and Learn*. London: Harper and Row.

Council for Awards in Child Care and Education (1991) *National Qualifications in Child Care and Education*. St Albans, Herts: CACHE.

Cox, M. (1992) *Children's Drawings*. London: Penguin.

Curtis, A. (1994) 'Play in different cultures and different childhoods', in J. Moyles (ed.) *The Excellence of Play*. Buckingham: Open University Press.

Davies, M. (1995) *Helping Children to Learn Through a Movement Perspective*. London: Hodder and Stoughton.

Department for Education (1995) *Art Programme of Study in the National Curriculum*. London: DfEE.

Department for Education and Employment in Conjunction with the School Curriculum and Assessment Authority (DfEE) (1996) *Desirable Outcomes for Children's Learning on Entry to Compulsory Education*. London: DfEE.

Department for Health and Social Security (1989) *The Children Act: Guidance and Regulations*, Volume 2. London: HMSO.

Edwards, C., Gandini, L. and Foreman, G. (eds) (1993) *The Hundred Languages of Children*. Norwood, NJ: Ablex Publishing Corporation.

Froebel, F. (1826) *The Education of Man*. New York: Appleton.

Gardner, H. (1980) *Artful Scribbles – The Significance of Children's Drawings*. London: Jill Norman.

Garvey, C. (1977) *Play*. London: Fontana.

Goldschmied, E. and Jackson, S. (1994) *People Under Three: Young Children in Day Care*. London: Routledge.

Gura, P. (ed.) (1992) *Exploring Learning: Young Children and Blockplay*. London: Paul Chapman.

Heckscher, A. (1966) 'The child's world: today and tomorrow', in H. Lewis (ed.) *Child Art at the Beginning of Self-Affirmation*. Berkeley, CA: Diabolo Press.

Her Majesty's Inspectorate (1989) *Aspects of Primary Education: The Education of Children Under Five*. London: HMSO.

Hutt, C. (1979) 'Play in the under fives: form, development and function', in J. G. Howells (ed.) *Modern Perspectives in the Psychiatry of Infancy*. New York: Bruner Marcel.

Isenberg, P. and Jalongo, M. (1993) *Creative Expression and Play in the Early Childhood Curriculum*. Englewood-Cliffs, NJ: Prentice-Hall.

Karmiloff-Smith, A. (1994) *Baby it's you*. London: Ebury Press.

Kellogg, R. (1970) *Analysing Children's Art*. Palo Alto, CA: Mayfield Publishing.

Kindler, A. (1995) 'Significance of adult input in early childhood artistic development', in C. M. Thompson (ed.) *The Visual Arts and Early Childhood*. Washington, DC: National Association for the Education of Children.

Lynch, M. (1992) *Creation Myths*. London: West London Institute of Higher Education.

Manser, S. (1995) *Artists in Residence: a Teacher's Handbook*. London Arts Board.

Matthews, J. (1994) *Helping Children to Draw and Paint in Early Childhood*. London: Hodder and Stoughton.

McDonald, T. and Simmons, G. (1989) *Musical Growth and Development*. New York: Schimer Books.

McKellar, P. (1957) *Imagination and Thinking: A Psychological Analysis*. London: Cohen and West.

Morgan, M. (1988) *Art 4–11*. Oxford: Blackwell.

Moyles, J. (1994) *The Excellence of Play*. Buckingham: Open University Press.

Moyles, J. (1989) *Just Playing?* Milton Keynes: Open University Press.

Nicholls, R. (ed.) (1986) *Rumpus Schema Extra*. Cleveland: Cleveland Teachers in Early Education.

Paley, V. G. (1988) *Bad Guys Don't Have Birthdays*. Chicago: University of Chicago Press.

Parnes, S. (1963) 'Development of individual creative talent', in C. W. Tylor and F. Barrons (eds) *Scientific Creativity: Its Recognition and Development*. New York: Wiley.

Piaget, J. (1926) *The Language and Thought of the Child*. London: Routledge and Kegan.

Piaget, J. (1951) *Play, Dreams and Imitations in Childhood*. London: Routledge and Kegan.

Pickering, J. (1976) 'Visual education for young children', in D. Brothwell (ed.) *Beyond Aesthetics: Investigations into the Nature of Visual Art*. London: Thames and Hudson.

Prentice, R. (1994) 'Experiential learning in play and art', in J. Moyles (ed.) *The Excellence of Play*. Buckingham: Open University Press.

Read, H. (1959) *Education Through Art*. London: Faber and Faber.

Richardson, M. (1948) *Art and the Child*. London: University of London Press.

School Curriculum and Assessment Authority (1996) *The National Curriculum*. London: HMSO.

Trevarthen, C. (1995) The child's need to learn a culture. *Children and Society*, 9, 1: 5–19.

Viola, W. (1937) *Child Art and Frank Cizek*. Austria: Austrian Junior Red Cross.

Vygotsky, L. (1978) *Mind in Society*. Cambridge, Mass.: Harvard University Press.

Weininger, O. (1988) ' "What if" and "as if" imagination and pretend play in early childhood', in K. Egan and D. Nadaner (ed.) *Imagination and Education*. New York: Teachers College Press.

Wilde, O. (1969) *Collected Works*. London: Dawson Pall Hall.

Winnicott, D. W. (1971) *Playing and Reality*. London: Tavistock.

Zohar, D. and Marshall, I. (1997) *Who's Afraid of Schrödinger's Cat?* London: Bloomsbury.

Index